The 70's Of Selection

... because drama belongs on TV... NOT in your love life. 😊

Jennifer

GET REAL, DITCH THE DRAMA, ENJOY DATING AGAIN

TANYA COOPER

Copyright © 2024 Tanya Cooper.

All rights reserved. No part of this publication may be reproduced, distributed, or transmitted in any form or by any means, including photocopying, recording, or other electronic or mechanical methods, without the prior written permission of the publisher, except in the case of brief quotations embodied in critical reviews and certain other noncommercial uses permitted by copyright law. For permission contact: tcooper@coopstrat.com.

ISBN: 979-8-99158321-3 (Paperback)
ISBN: 979-8-9915832-0-6 (Hardcover)
ISBN: 979-8-9915832-2-0 (EBook)
ISBN: 979-8-9915832-6-8 (Audio)

Any references to historical events, real people, or real places are used fictitiously. Names, characters, and places are products of the author's imagination.

The trademarks, service marks, and slogans referenced in this book are owned by third parties. All references to third-party trademarks, creative works, and individuals/celebrities are fair use and fall within the scope of First Amendment protections. No affiliation with, endorsement by, or sponsorship by any of those third-party trademark owners, claimants, authors, or individuals/celebrities is claimed or otherwise suggested.

Book design by SelfPublishing.com
Editing by SelfPublishing.com

First printing edition 2024.

Please leave a review!

I'd love to connect with you!

Scan here for your free gift!

https://www.instagram.com/playersmeetyourcoach/

To learn more visit

https://www.playersmeetyourcoach.com

Dedication

First, to the true loves of my life... my sons, thank you for showing me the true meaning of unconditional love. With you, life is always an adventure. May your lives be blessed with as much love, or greater, as you have shown me in mine.

To their father, thank you for jumping off that ledge with me to create both of them when we were just kids ourselves. It was the best choice I've ever made in my life. I'm forever grateful for all the memories we've created with our family and for our continued friendship.

Lastly, to all other members of my inner circle (especially my Aunt Nicole), thank you for always being there to talk to and for your ongoing love and support. It's been a wild ride and there's still so much left to do. Looking forward to wherever our next adventures take us.

Contents

Introduction xi
Chapter 1: The Ugly You 1
Chapter 2: What Do You Want? Be Honest! 15
Chapter 3: The First "C": Chemistry 29
Chapter 4: The Second "C": Compatibility 37
Chapter 5: The Third "C": Conflict 51
Chapter 6: The Fourth "C": Communication 75
Chapter 7: The Fifth "C": Community 87
Chapter 8: The Sixth "C": Commitment 99
Chapter 9: The Seventh "C": Choices 118
Chapter 10: Love: Fantasy or Force? 130
Chapter 11: Ugliness is in the Eyes of the Beholder 142
Glossary 153

Introduction

Navigating the world of romance can often feel like an emotional rollercoaster, filled with exhilarating highs and gut-wrenching lows. As someone who has experienced the complexities of dating firsthand, I understand the challenges that come with finding a meaningful connection.

It's easy to get lost in the whirlwind of attraction and desire, only to find ourselves grappling with heartbreak or disappointment. This book is born out of my desire to transform those painful experiences into something positive, constructive, and humorous. After all, sometimes you just need a good laugh.

On my journey, I discovered a framework that has helped me approach dating with greater clarity and intention: The Seven C's of Selection. These attributes—Chemistry, Compatibility, Conflict, Communication, Community, Commitment, and Choice—offer a way to evaluate potential partners and build healthier, more fulfilling relationships. Central to this process is the importance of embracing your true self. Hiding your authentic self can lead to superficial connections and heartache. By being open and honest about who you are, you invite deeper understanding and more genuine relationships.

By understanding and applying these concepts, I hope to empower you to make your romantic journey not just enjoyable, but also rewarding. Together, we'll explore how to harness the wisdom gleaned from past experiences, ensuring that each step in your quest for love is as enriching as it is meaningful.

Let's turn the heartache into hope, and embark on a path toward enjoyable connections.

CHAPTER 1

The Ugly You

If you're hoping this book will tell you what you need to do to "get your perfect man" or that it will say exactly "what girls want," you should stop reading right here. If you're looking for a book that will provide guidance on how to contort yourself into something more attractive to the opposite sex, you're shit out of luck. This isn't the book for you!

It won't help you project an "image" that will entice someone into wanting you, or help you with tips on thinking or acting like anyone but yourself. This book is intended to show you why you have a better chance at love when you embrace and display your "*ugly*" parts, than you do by projecting all of your alleged "*great*" characteristics.

We've all heard someone say, "I want to be loved unconditionally." Ok, great. But can *you* love someone unconditionally? Do you even know what that entails? How many times have you met someone and said," Wow, I just love that guy's hairy armpits and the way he scratches his balls when he's watching television"? Maybe you love it when your girl has a complete emotional breakdown when you leave town for a business meeting and she proceeds to continually blow up your phone. Isn't it fun to be constantly accused of having an affair because you didn't text her back in less than thirty seconds?

What?

These aren't the qualities that make you want to fall madly and deeply in love with someone? Shocking.

The fact of the matter is that it is easy to love someone when all you see are their good qualities and you only experience good times. Not to mention, whenever you are together, they are always well-groomed, emotionally stable, secure about themselves and confident in your relationship. However, real love, the kind that withstands the tests of time, is not based on all that "good stuff." Real love, some might even use the term "unconditional love," is when you've seen how ugly someone can be but you *choose* to love them anyway.

You accept their obsessive compulsivity. Their temper tantrums. Their emotional breakdowns. Their hairy crotch. Their bad odor. Their snoring. Their inability to cook and even their inability to lick your vagina properly. Why? Because in some respects, those things just aren't important to you. Maybe you've reasoned their other qualities outweigh their bad qualities, so you're willing to accept all that bad oral sex.

Over time, you've probably developed a deep understanding of your partner. They also understand themselves. You both accept that, although there is a lot of beauty in one another, there is also a certain amount of *ugly* existing in all of us. Whether you like it or not, you have to accept those ugly parts too. In short, you learn to love *the ugly you* and you also learn to love *the ugly them*.

Once you've mastered this, the game changes. You no longer fear that your undesirable qualities will be exposed. You stop being insecure about your ugly parts, and work toward understanding them. You change what you feel compelled to change, and embrace what you can't. Most importantly, you stop letting these ugly parts have power over your happiness. You stop feeding fear. You stop letting your ugliness cause you to self-destruct or sabotage your relationships. You stop hiding this important part of yourself from potential love interests, and learn to love yourself, even the "ugly" parts. You accept them. You become stronger.

Do you remember the movie *8 Mile*? If you've never seen the movie, in short, it's set in the Detroit area, intended to depict a young rapper named "B-Rabbit" trying to make it big. In the movie, there are many scenes showing various rap battles. The winner is usually the person who had the best delivery, audience response, and wittiest insults directed toward their competitor.

In previous attempts, the young rapper literally choked during these rap battles. He let the other rapper's insults get to him. However, by the end of the movie, he rises to the occasion by openly embracing his *ugly*. He walks up on stage, knowing the other rapper is about to rip him apart and expose all of his perceived insecurities. After winning the coin toss, B-Rabbit gets to rap first. His next move is pure genius.

What does he do? He takes away his competitor's power. How? B-Rabbit rips into *himself*. He exposes all of his insecurities *first*. He openly insults himself in front of the crowd, and something amazing happens: it renders his competitor speechless, taking away his power. What previously tore B-Rabbit down, has now placed him in a position of strength. It empowered him and he won the battle. The crowd loved it. The other rapper couldn't even formulate a sentence. He just walked off the stage.

So, why am I talking about rap battles? It's a good example of embracing your ugly parts and not allowing someone else's narrative to have power over you. More often than not, it can be a person's attempt to paint themselves in a positive light while making you feel like an ugly duck... or an ugly B-Rabbit.

For example, how many times have you heard a man say, "I don't like drama" when referring to a woman's actions? "Drama," also known as an emotional outburst, is something that occurs *because* we are *human!* Why would women allow men to shame them out of having emotions to make their experience more pleasant? Having emotions is not negative. Perhaps the extent of a woman's display of emotions can be ugly, but I guess it all depends on the participants.

Let's break this down a little further.

Let's say you're a guy and you meet a woman who you think is hot. She's so hot you want to have sex with her as soon as possible. It's understandable. Physical attraction and sexuality are normal responses. However, what you need to understand is that in many cases, having sex with a woman is like getting a deal.

A deal?

Yes.

Like a bargain. A "two for one" to be more precise. Now you might be saying, "oh, I like deals." Great, but depending on your level of emotional maturity and emotional availability, you might not like *this* bargain.

What I'm referring to is that when you take a woman's vagina, you may also take her heart. Now this might not occur overnight, but the next day, when you decide not to text her, just know you're quickly falling into the realm of "fuckboy." A couple more hours pass and you still don't text her or tell her that you want to see her again? Ok, Casper, way to ghost her.

On the other side of this exchange, she's constantly checking her phone and going over everything you said to her last night. You made it sound like you wanted a serious relationship. You said you were open to having a girlfriend. Hours have passed. Now, an entire day! Still nothing? The realization that she was *nothing* to you sets in, and the unraveling starts.

The feelings of being used and disrespected are felt all the way to her thumbs. Before you know it, she is rapid fire texting you. Your phone is legit blowing up! You're used to it, though. It happens to you all the time. It's part of getting laid by chicks that don't want to be casual.

Ding! Ding! Ding! Here we go…

> Her: I really enjoyed spending time with you last night. I can't wait until we can do it again.

> Her: Hope you're having a great day so far. Any plans for tonight?

> Her: Hello?

> Her: I'm thinking about you right now 😈

> Her: I thought you said you liked me?

> Her: Are you ghosting me? You said you weren't into one-night stands! You got all offended when I said you gave off fuckboy vibes... I knew it! Everything you said was just bs to get into bed. Mr. "I'm not that kind of guy." Now you just ghost? You're such a fucking child. How could you do this when I was very clear about not wanting to be used for sex? I told you I'm not into casual! I am not your free escort!

> Her: You weren't even that good and as for your penis, I've swallowed vitamins that were bigger.

> Her: I left my socks at your place. I'm coming to get them.

Before you can even leave your house, you hear your doorbell and she's standing in front of your camera! You can hear her crying, and shouting, and knocking, and saying, "You are a horrible, despicable asshole! How could you do this to me? How could you use me? If you think I'm disposable after one use, you're dead wrong!"

Now, you're sitting there telling yourself that she is bat shit crazy. She might be, but perhaps you should've spent more time last night exploring her emotional stability, instead of her vagina. Maybe she's not crazy, though. Maybe *you're* crazy for expecting that you can deceive women like this. Maybe this is a common response when someone feels lied to and betrayed.

If you, indeed, gave the impression that you didn't sleep around and were looking for a serious relationship, then own your part in the situation you've contributed to creating. You should have told her the truth: You were just looking for casual encounters.

You get yourself ready to open the door. You have your speech all prepared. You've given it more times than you can count. Calling her a crazy, psycho bitch and threatening to call the police will get you out of this. It's highly effective to turn the conversation around and make it all about her reaction. After all, that's better than calling yourself a liar.

Wait, weren't you the one that said you wanted to have "drama-free" encounters with women? Turns out that lying to them doesn't make that possible. Shocking!

If, by some miracle, you are successful in convincing her to believe she is crazy to expect common courtesy and honesty, don't pat yourself on the back. For all you men out there that want to have a drama-free, stable and secure woman in your life at some point in your future, don't create drama. You need to understand that *you* are contributing to the problem when *you* conduct yourselves in this manner. Your expectations are unrealistic.

What is realistic is to expect that a woman has emotions, and that if she opens up to you, allowing you to physically penetrate her vagina, you probably also have a straight shot at her heart. I'm not saying this will happen in every case, but it's not an infrequent occurrence. If you want sex without emotion, fuck a blow-up doll, a hole in the wall or a warm apple pie! Fuck anything inanimate, but don't fuck a woman.

Simple. Problem solved. No drama. A pie can't talk back to you; and it doesn't have fingers so it can't text you. It also can't place expectations on you or ask you to define your intentions or your relationship goals. A pie also can't drive to your house.

Women, on the other hand, are human beings. It's a well-known, scientific fact that humans have emotions. Emotions are not ugly. That is just a label that certain people impose on displays of emotion to absolve themselves from treating others, women in this case, with empathy, courtesy and respect.

Now, women are not blameless in this exchange. If you are looking for a good man to share your life with, then what the hell were you doing with a loser that just fucks you and can't even text you back? He could text you incessantly for hours leading up to your meeting but all of a sudden, his thumbs fall off after that orgasm and now you don't exist. Now, you just represent "pressure," "expectations," and "drama."

Fuck him, and fuck you! Oh, he did; but girl, *you* allowed it to happen.

Yes, I understand. You want to find your person and see the good in people. You want to believe you are special enough for them to choose you as a partner, but you don't need them to validate your self-worth. Especially if you know that your self-worth is hanging on by a thread and you can't take any more rejection. In fact, more rejection might just cause you to come unglued and let your inner psycho out.

If this is where you're at, then maybe you need to date different people than your girlfriend, Roxanne, who just got divorced and wants "no strings attached" sex. In your case, if you give sex away before finding out what a person's intentions are or if they are emotionally available, you may be hurting yourself unnecessarily. A better approach for you might be to stop and evaluate a few things other than just chemistry.

What else do you want to know about them when you do the "walk of shame" tomorrow, still wearing the same dress that you showed up in? Will you be hiding your face as you walk out with your hair sporting that "Just Fucked" look and your make-up looking like you just took a hot yoga class?

Are you going to spend the rest of the day wondering if they will text you or call you? Do you wonder if that is all they wanted? Were you just another patient in their waiting room? Things got pretty hot. What if they do this with everyone? Do they have any diseases? You didn't even ask about their dating history. You start realizing you know nothing about them, but somehow you went home with them, slept with them, and spent the night.

Again, there is nothing wrong with this if you have the mental and emotional capacity to handle this type of exchange—and take appropriate precautions. If sex was all you were looking for and you are ok with it, then good for you. If you don't care if you ever hear from or see them again, great. You got what you wanted. You get a gold star and a shit ton of orgasms! Woo hoo!

However, if you are not someone that can do casual relationships, making someone wait for sex isn't going to harm you. The worst thing that could happen is they show you they're not really interested; and you save yourself from finding that out *after* you slept with them.

If you can identify with the man in this situation and you are constantly finding yourself in a sea of drama after most of your one-night stands, who's fault is that? You lie to them because you know you want that nurturing, girlfriend energy; you just don't want the girl to hang around afterward. You've convinced yourself that women who are ok with being casual don't treat you as good. They don't care as much about you. You want girlfriend vibes and privileges, without the strings.

Unfortunately, after each encounter, you're always left with the task of ghosting them. You're always left wondering if they're going to be *cool* and allow you to compartmentalize the exchange, or if they're going to come unglued. Sometimes you don't completely ghost them, you breadcrumb them.

Breadcrumbing means that you text them from time to time in the hopes of keeping them as an option to exercise when you're feeling lonely or horny. You just don't want the obligation of spending time with them or committing to them. You know if you tell them that, they will not want to have sex with you.

The result is neither person will feel positive about this experience. They will both blame one another. She will call him a lying fuck boy, and he will refer to her as a crazy psycho bitch. However, the simple truth is neither of them evaluated one another on anything more than *chemistry* or physical traits.

This is how a lot of people navigate the process of dating. Dating apps don't really help you in this regard either.

What if you spent some time revealing your ugly and learning about their ugly? If you had, maybe they wouldn't be balls deep into you on their kitchen counter five minutes into your "Netflix and Chill" date. Imagine for a moment that instead of agreeing to a "no effort" date, you insisted on meeting them for coffee, drinks, or dinner in a public place. A place where you could do the most radical thing… talk. Holy crap! What a concept!

If you are always preaching "character counts" to your besties, please tell me what you learned about this man while he was treating your vagina like a backed up toilet.

Making the decision to be intimate with someone based on chemistry is very common. We've all been here. For most of us, probably more than once. But what if you were consciously aware of other factors to consider?

What if you *communicated* prior to this night and found out whether or not you were *compatible*. Perhaps during this chat, you could ask some pointed questions and highlight their *conflict* resolution skills, or lack thereof. What if they tell you about their friends and family, and you learn a whole lot about the *community* they surround themselves with.

If the conversation was flowing and the drinks were good, you might have even learned about their relationship goals and their views on *commitment*. At least once during this exchange you'd be sure to learn about some of the *choices* they've made in their lives that brought them to you today.

Finding the right person to spend extended time with can be difficult. To be more descriptive, I've always felt it was like dragging a rhinoceros uphill in the mud wearing stilettos and a pencil skirt.

Where do you start looking? The world is a large place. It can be like finding a specific fish in the Seven Seas during a tsunami where the water is tumultuous, as well as unpredictable.

That may sound exhausting; or maybe it sounds adventurous. It all depends on what type of person you are. It also depends on what you want, how you approach it, and how honest you are about who you are.

Do you bring your authentic self to dates or do you send your alter ego, aka your sales representative? Do you represent your authentic self or do you hide the things that you are insecure about? Do you conceal facts and information that would probably make them reject you?

What will *you* be evaluating *them* on and, in return, what will *they* evaluate *you* on? Surely there's something more than looks and sex to consider.

I was on a quest to figure out how to make the process easier, more enjoyable and honest in the hopes it would produce better results for myself and others. As I thought about the Seven Seas, it hit me that maybe there are *Seven C's* associated with selecting someone to date. After some further thought, the picture clarified itself to me. There could be *Seven C's of Selection* such as:

1. Chemistry
2. Compatibility
3. Conflict
4. Communication
5. Community
6. Commitment
7. Choice

In the following chapters, I'm going to talk about what these mean, and why they're important factors in understanding yourself so that you can be more authentic in your relationships, and hopefully get what you want: a better match and more positive encounters. This means, however, you will need to be brutally honest about what it is that you actually *want*. So, before we dive into the C's, let's talk about that first.

CHAPTER 2

What Do You Want? Be Honest!

What do you want? It's a pretty common thing people might ask when meeting a new love interest. When they ask this question, they are usually asking what you want out of this encounter. How often are you honest when answering them? More importantly, how often are you honest when answering yourself? Maybe deep down you know what you want but you'd never voice it right out of the gate. Worse yet, maybe you're ashamed to even acknowledge it to yourself.

Why the hell wouldn't you? How are you going to get what you want if you can't even verbalize it?

To illustrate this point, let's say, you are someone who wants low effort, NSA (No Strings Attached) sex. How often do you actually tell someone, "I want to have sex with you without buying you drinks or dinner. I want you to come to my house, hang out, have sex, and leave. Afterward, I don't want to text you or see you again until I'm horny"?

Perhaps you're someone who doesn't want to support yourself financially. You have no desire to work hard or at all. You're a proud sugar baby and that's all you want to be. You want a luxury lifestyle that someone else provides for you. Bring on the sugar mommies and daddies! You've never been good about paying your bills. Essentially you can't feed or clothe yourself on your own, and you don't ever want to.

Do you tell your new love interest that you're a financial disaster, have no intention of ever financially supporting yourself, or holding down a full-time job? Do you tell them that their bank account is probably one of the most important things to you?

Maybe you are someone who is ultra-needy and you want to be the center of someone's universe. You want them to come straight home after work and hold you, talk to you, and pet you like a lap dog. You are a clingy, attention-seeking child and you love being that way. They can't go work out or visit their friends and family. All of their spare time needs to be focused on you.

Are you telling them on your first date that all of your prior relationships failed because your needs have to come before theirs? Do you let them know that when this doesn't happen, you have an emotional melt-down and you cry like a baby until you get your own way?

Another example could be that you just recently took a new job in another state and left your spouse and four kids back in your home state. You told your spouse you wanted to go alone first to get situated in your new job. You further reason that this approach will better position you to find a new place for you all to live. You agree they will join you after the school year is finished. However, this wasn't true. The truth is you're bored with your life and with them. You want renewed passion but you're afraid to say that.

So, instead of telling them what you want, you intentionally lie to them to get some time away. Given it is only January, you've realized that this new job and your lies have given you almost six months to get some fresh meat. Do you tell all the new candidates that you're meeting on your dating app that you're married and just looking for sex? Or, do you conceal that and make them unknowing side pieces in your marriage?

So, this seems like an appropriate time to remind y'all this book is definitely not going to help you out with dating etiquette or getting laid. The whole purpose of this book was to help people be honest with themselves so that they can clarify and embrace their likes and dislikes. More importantly, it's intended to help you be transparent about what it is that you want.

In my humble, unsubstantiated opinion, knowing yourself and what you want might help you make better choices for *you*. This may also help you be more direct and efficient with potential love interests and where you spend your time.

This is another way of saying create less "drama," which could also result in breaking less hearts, including your own. Unless you like creating drama and breaking hearts; then, by all means, carry on. However, if you're interested in having greater peace, joy, and positive interactions, then figuring out and expressing what you want is critical.

With that in mind, let's explore other scenarios defining what you want. One of those things is likely defining your relationship goals. Do you want to be in a serious relationship or do you just want something casual? Perhaps you don't know the answer. So, how would you answer that question if it were posed to you?

Why is this important? Simple. If your goal is to try to minimize drama and find other people that you vibe with, you might consider giving this some serious thought in your selection process. Let me try to demonstrate with some more examples.

Let's say that you're older, you've been divorced for years and have all the kids you ever want to have. You're an empty nester. You've already experimented with different love interests and know what you're looking for. For years you've done the work on yourself to become emotionally available. You've never been more ready for commitment.

You're dating with the intention of finding someone to have a serious relationship with, preferably someone without kids or pets. You want to travel freely with your partner. You hope this will happen in the very near future. At this stage of your life, you're dating with intention and probably not looking to waste time.

However, someone else's situation may be different. Someone else may have just gotten out of a long-term relationship and now they're interested in trying out a few different things to figure out what they really want in their next partner. They just want sex and companionship. They're not emotionally able to have more than that right now.

If these two people swipe right and jump into bed together without talking about what they want out of this exchange, it's probably not going to meet either of their needs. You can clearly see that there's a huge potential for conflict because they have incompatible relationship goals. They are also not at the same place in their lives.

So, it seems important to know what your relationship goals are and where you are in your personal journey. Things seemingly run much smoother, romantically speaking, if you try to interact with others who have compatible relationship goals.

Right about now you might be thinking, "Wait a minute, lady! Is this another book about waiting ninety days before having sex?" The answer is, no. This is not one of those books. However, you might want to have a simple conversation to find out if you and your new love interest are on the same page before allowing yourself to be pounded into the kitchen counter.

After all, your kitty is complicated. You don't want to end up bitter that you went down on him for ten minutes but all he did was spit on your kitty before diving in. Telling each other what you want, at least sexually, could've made this a better experience from the start.

Perhaps you're someone who needs to watch videos of penguins in bikinis before you get turned on. So, there's no way ninety seconds is enough time for you to be ready for sex. The good parts on the videos don't start until at least five minutes in.

Maybe you were cringing all throughout the latest sexual encounter, but at the same time you also gave him credit for being a great gym partner. Even though he's terrible in bed, you reasoned that since you started dating him, your ass has never looked this good. So, you just grabbed the apples in the bowl next to the dirty plates on his counter and waited for it to be over.

You made sure to moan at the appropriate times all while visualizing LL Cool J in his place. *Side Note: If you don't like LL Cool J, then you can obviously insert whoever makes your kitty purr. No pun intended. However, this is my book. So, hellloooo LL!*

The point is, in this latter scenario, you prioritized having a great looking ass over your sexual enjoyment in the bedroom... or kitchen. So, asking yourself "What do I want sexually" seems to be an essential part of the journey. It's all about you and what you *really* want. Be honest with yourself *and* your love interests. If you don't know what you want, there's nothing wrong with that, but embrace that stance and be transparent about it with potential love interests.

If you do know what you want, then own it and more importantly, *communicate* what that is. All of it. Don't hold back anything.

Let's stay on this topic. Maybe you are just DTF (that's a technical term for "Down to Fuck"). Again, who cares? If that's what you want, then that is what you want. Maybe you just flew into Miami for a fun weekend with your friends and you're looking for some locals to show you a good time, give you free sex, and pay for your drinks.

Here's a big newsflash for you, though. Not all of the locals want to be your sugar mommies, daddies, or free escorts! So, remember that. Next time you are swiping through your dating app on your party weekend, maybe don't "swipe right" on all the people that listed "looking for a serious relationship" on their profile.

You have to be honest with yourself. If you're just using the dating app as a means to obtain free escort services for the weekend, let people know. Or maybe don't be so cheap and pay a professional for it. I tell my best friend all the time that if I were an escort, it would cost $62.50 just to lick my ankle. So, if you quantify that value over the total area of my body, it would be an expensive night. I've got *a lot* of area.

Here's another one. You like watching your partner have sex with other people. Ok. Cool. Find someone that understands that lifestyle or is open to learning about it. Don't try to convert someone that is not interested. Whatever you do, don't make them feel like there's something wrong with them and label them a prude because they aren't meeting your specific sexual needs. They might just like romantic, missionary-style sex. Again, there's nothing wrong with that. It's just *different* from cuckolding fetishes. Things will be more enjoyable if you find someone who embraces that quality about you.

Up until now, your approach has been to hide these things from your potential love interests. You don't address it until one day you realize that they are attracted to you and are *catching feelings*. Only then do you spring it on them. Maybe you're thinking that now that they have feelings for you, they won't ditch your ass when they find out you've deceived them about who you truly are.

The question is, who did they develop feelings for? You, or the version of yourself you pretended to be?

Now, there's a chance that the things you concealed aren't really that important to them, and therefore, they won't care. However, what if they do? It's probably not going to bring you closer together. I mean, can you imagine that conversation three months into your new relationship? "Uh, hey boo, ummm I was thinking we could spice things up tonight so I invited my friend Chad over to have sex with you while I sit on a chair and watch. Cool?"

Get the picture? Call me crazy, but this might have been better discussed earlier on. Clearly your sexual desires will not be met and your love interest could eventually grow tired of never satisfying you.

Another scenario that seems very prevalent could arise when you are unraveling from a live-in relationship. Your soon-to-be-ex is still living in your house and you are lonely and need to have sex. Again, cool. Just don't lie to your potential love interests. Don't tell them the reason they can't come to your house is because your kids are there on an extended visit.

It's obviously going to look suspicious when you say you can leave your kids in the house unattended on nights when you're horny. They're going to think either you're a terrible parent or you're hiding something. Either way, you're probably becoming less attractive by the minute.

They're also going to figure it out when the only time you call them is while you're at work, driving somewhere, or walking your dog at night. You didn't want to tell your new love interest that you're in a bad relationship, because you're horny and your ego is in the toilet. You know you won't get laid if you tell the truth.

You're also not attracted to the other options that would accept casual sex. They seem promiscuous. You want those nurturing girlfriend privileges. So, you deceive this great new person who is totally into you. You pull out all your lines and games to get them to be attracted to you, to like you.

Then, something predictable happened. Your new option has, in fact, fallen for you and you get laid. Mission accomplished! Wow! But wait. Oh no! They like you, and now they want to come to your house and get to know you better. How terrible of them!

Now you've got a situation because you've recently fallen back in bed with your "soon-to-be ex". Your family has also been encouraging you to reconcile. Now what do you do with your new love interest? That's right! Ghost them!

Except that doesn't work. Now they're blowing up your phone, wondering what happened.

You've made them feel exactly how your soon-to-be-ex was making you feel… like a piece of shit. Congratulations! How great was it using this person to fill your voids and feed your ego? How nice of you to make someone else pay for the shit in your current relationship. How spectacular of you to gaslight them and make this conflict all about their reaction.

Their reaction was totally normal, by the way. They were understandably hurt. *You* created this drama in your own life. Own that shit! You could've been honest and pursued people who were only interested in a casual encounter with you. However, your ego couldn't take it. You wanted wifey benefits with free escort responsibilities.

The truth is, you weren't emotionally available for a relationship. You were also probably on the rebound. Why couldn't you just put your ego aside and spit it out? Say it!

"I'm an emotional mess right now."

"I'm bitter!"

"I just want to spend time with you when it suits my schedule and my needs."

"I don't care about what you want."

"I just want to be single and fuck."

OK! Go get it! No one is judging you.

You want to know why you couldn't tell the other person this? Probably because you can't bring yourself to accept that this is who you really are.

You can't handle your own truth and perceived ugliness. So, how could anyone else? You'd rather see yourself as a great person who's honest, nice, and treats people well. That's the story you tell yourself. That's the image you want to project.

The truth is, you're not that person right now. Maybe it's temporary and the old you will come back. But right now, while you are going through this situation in your relationship, you are broken. Your ego is shattered. You're filled with anger and have huge voids to fill. This most recent tryst was nothing more to you than something to absorb all of your own negative emotions.

Lucky them. They got to be your bad energy sponge. The sooner you see yourself for who you really are, the better you can communicate your real wants to someone else. If you're saying to yourself that being honest might have resulted in you being alone… maybe that's not a bad thing for you right now.

On the flip side, if you are the person on the other side of this equation, you're probably pretty angry. You've been single for a long time and you're over it. You wanted this to materialize quickly into a long-term relationship. You didn't really care about asking too many questions. You just wanted a warm body in your bed!

So, the first person that you met after this epiphany got love bombed by you. Asking more questions could have possibly brought their situation to light. However, you've *always* been like this. You turn on your "super wife" persona and try to lock shit down. Feeling smothered, your love interests usually hastily run from you, fearful of being dragged back to your cave and held hostage for the *rest of their lives*. They ghost you, and you're left wondering what you did wrong.

You were showering them with affection. Why did they run from you? The problem here is that you had an objective which was to get into a long-term, committed relationship, stat. An objective that you didn't voice or discuss to see if they wanted the same thing.

The point I'm making is that when you are honest with yourself about *what you want*, you can be honest with others. You will consciously look for someone whose relationship goals and wants are compatible with yours. This seems far more harmonious than trying to attract people to the image of yourself that you feel better about projecting.

There are people out there right now that won't mind a casual tryst. There are also people that want to be in committed relationships, as well as those that don't know what the hell they want. Wouldn't it feel much better to interact with another person who really understands you? Imagine how much better your encounters would be if you met a person that was in the same situation as you.

> Compatible Goals = Minimal Drama
> = Greater Enjoyment for All

So, get comfortable with what you want and accept that about yourself. Communicate it to potential romantic partners. More importantly, take some time to assess whether the object of your affection feels the same. It's not all about you! There's another person in the equation with a separate agenda. It might be a surprising realization for some of you, but other people weren't put on this earth just to serve all your needs and desires.

Understanding and accepting that the object of your affection may not be in the same place as you are with your journey is a *peace protector*. If your love interest wants something different than you do, you have to decide whether that's something you're willing to accept. If not, then be transparent about it and move on.

Neither of you are wrong. You're just different and want different things. Different is okay. It might not make you compatible, but it doesn't make you, or anyone else, a horrible despicable asshole.

Selecting a person that you can create positive moments and memories with is not an easy task. There's so much to consider. In these first couple of chapters, we've already created more awareness about our insecurities and the importance of knowing what we want. What else should we be thinking about?

This is where the Seven C's of Selection makes its entrance. Think of these C's as points of consideration to help enhance your selection process. While we will not all prioritize them the same, we can all use them to enhance our selection process. So, hold onto your hormones, folks! And let's dive into the first C that we usually can't control. Chemistry.

CHAPTER 3

The First "C": Chemistry

Ahhhh. Good ol' chemistry. Maybe you liked chemistry class or maybe you didn't. Regardless of your stance on the class, you probably don't mind having ten orgasms in one afternoon! It's certainly better than the alternative of not having them or feeling the need to fake them.

Chemistry is often the first "C" we encounter.

In this chapter, I'm using the word "chemistry" to talk mostly about physical attraction and sex. We've actually talked a lot about chemistry already. There's no denying that we've all experienced it at some point in our lives. We see a person from across a room or maybe just their photo on a dating app, and something warm and tingly starts happening between our legs. Chemistry. We're attracted.

For some people, this weighs very heavily on the "finding a mate" spectrum (there is no *spectrum*... I made that up). Let's face it, sex is natural and, for a lot of people, it is an important part of attraction. We preferably want to be turned on by our romantic partners. It goes without saying that the sexual part of a relationship is easier when both people are attracted and turned on by one another; when there is chemistry.

Have you ever asked yourself, why, at the beginning of a relationship, is sex so good? Why does it wear off? There are many reasons and factors, one of which is the chemical oxytocin. Oxytocin is also referred to as the "love hormone." Now don't get your panties in a bunch. I'm not going to get all technical and give a science lesson. Trust me, it wouldn't be much of a lesson.

Where was I? Oh yes, chemistry. There are some fundamental things that occur in our bodies that we might not have control over, and one of them is a hormone called "oxytocin."

Oxytocin, often dubbed the "love hormone," plays an important role in influencing our chemical reaction to someone. In a study led by Dr. Helen Fisher, she explored how oxytocin fosters emotional bonding and attachment. This hormone can lead individuals to make swift, often irrational choices in love.

When oxytocin levels rise—triggered by intimacy and physical closeness—people may find themselves more vulnerable to falling head over heels for someone. This chemical response can create a powerful desire to connect, often overriding rational decision-making and leading to spontaneous romantic encounters. Said differently, when your oxytocin levels rise, you're most likely not considering long-term implications of your current decisions.[1]

Its effects don't last forever, though, and when they wear off, you're left with the burning question, "Can I stand this person?" More importantly, "Can I stand having them as *my* person?"

When oxytocin finally wears off, you've entered a different phase. It might also end up being where you ask yourself, "What the fuck was I thinking?" The answer, oxytocin. That's what you were thinking. So, in other words, you weren't thinking. You were chemically reacting, like baking soda and vinegar.

With chemistry, knowing what you want seemingly becomes more instinctual and reactive, rather than being a well-thought out plan. You may easily find yourself in a

---

[1] Fisher, H. E. (1998). Lust, attraction, and attachment in mammalian reproduction. *Human Nature*, 9(1), 23-52. https://doi.org/10.1007/s12110-998-1010-5

situation where you are instantly attracted without knowing anything else about someone.

For example, maybe you like tall, muscular, dark-haired men with chiseled jaw-lines. Maybe you like short curvy red-headed women with big lips and green eyes. Maybe you like women with ponytails and stilettos with legs that go on for days, or maybe you like bald headed, gym bros in those gray jogging pants. Perhaps you like big, bold, and bootylicious librarians, lumberjacks, men in uniform, IT geeks, or as mentioned previously, penguins in bikinis. Again, you like what you like and that's it.

If appearance is important to you, and it drives your chemical reaction, sexually speaking, there's very little you can do about that. You are doing yourself a disservice by trying to choose someone that you are only mildly attracted to because they make great omelets in the morning, or have a great job and can provide for you financially.

As I've said before, and maybe I should say it every chapter, I am no relationship expert. I know more of "what not to do" than "what to do" in a relationship. Nevertheless, after many failed relationships, situationships and *textationships* (yes, that's a thing), I've learned a thing or two. I've also come to realize that that old cliché "love is not enough" is quite accurate.

Just think about it. If love were enough, then why do people break up and experience pain? Then, the very next day, they find themselves texting their ex for something made up and stupid, like returning a plastic food container? Do you think that they seriously *needed* to meet to return the orange stained food container that they could've easily replaced at any store for less than $3? Probably not. Yet, before you know it, you accidentally (on purpose) meet up and have sex with them.

These past few years, looking back on my dating history, I've realized for decades I made the same mistakes over and over and *over* and *over* again. Don't judge me. I'm a *slow* learner. I would constantly choose the wrong person based on initial chemistry. I gravely overlooked deal-breaking habits and traits in my love interests. I didn't spend enough time getting to know *myself* and what made *me* happy. To be honest, the sex wasn't even that great most of the time. It was just comfortable to have someone around that I could have regular sex with.

I didn't realize, until I was much older, that I should be evaluating a person on a lot more than chemistry. The most *fascinating* thing was I didn't realize I was doing it. I knew that how I was choosing love interests wasn't working, but I couldn't figure out what I needed to do differently. Then it hit me. I was only evaluating them on chemistry before investing emotionally.

Now, I'm an accountant and generally pretty logical. However, passion was the one area where my logic and reason took a back seat. If I was looking for someone for more than just sex, then I needed to consciously ensure that I evaluated more facets of an individual before deciding on whether that person should be allowed access to me. Yes, I said *allowed access*. Because not everyone should get that privilege.

Not everyone *should be* allowed access to you and have the opportunity to disrupt your peace. I realized that I didn't place enough value on my time or myself. I hadn't clearly defined what I wanted. I also totally missed the part where that other person came in with their own agenda. I was focused only on what I wanted at that moment. Also, based on my prior experiences and examples, I expected that relationships came with a lot of conflict. I didn't realize that I could minimize that upfront by refraining from attaching to someone until the chemistry phase cooled down.

Let's go through some examples. Have you ever seen someone and thought, "This person is soooo hot!" Then ended up in bed with them and they were terrible? While they were on top of you, you literally noticed all of the paint imperfections on the ceiling of their bedroom. At one point, you had a whole conversation in your head. It probably went something like this:

While staring at the ceiling, you thought to yourself, "Maybe their tongue has a birth defect? How can anyone be that uncoordinated naturally? Poor thing. Just try to be encouraging."

After that night, you ghost them. It doesn't matter that they were a former pro football player or the CEO of a fortune 500 company. It doesn't matter that they live in a mansion in Malibu and drive a luxury car. You just can't imagine having sex with that person *ever* again. Even if your beloved Aunt Nicole tells you that some people can be taught; you already know that this is not a project you want to tackle. So, you move on.

You find that you're meeting people that are good in bed, but they don't have the other qualities you want in a partner. Then there are those that you've met and have great chemistry with, but they don't want to be in a relationship. They're just looking for casual sex and companionship.

Conversely, you may find that you've met people that have those *other* qualities you want, but they're terrible in bed or don't match your sex drive. You just can't seem to find it all in one person.

So, how much should we rely on chemistry? There's no definite answer to this question. It depends how it ranks in your life. Only *you* can determine how much or how little chemistry ranks in your selection process. If it ranks very highly, then you need to be honest with yourself and others about it. If it's a small factor for you, then what else should you be considering?

Only you can answer these questions. Knowing yourself and being mindful that you need more than just chemistry could be a game changer. If you fall into the category of "needing more than just sex" and yet you don't look at other aspects of your love interest's character before emotionally investing, you may be in for a rough ride (no pun intended). Especially after the chemicals wear off.

After a few weeks of multiple orgasms and skipping work to spend days in bed with your new love interest, you might want to get back to *normal* life. This is usually where we start to notice other aspects about our new love interest, like our next "C," compatibility, or lack thereof.

Take a breath, cool your loins, and let's talk about some things that you might have more control over.

CHAPTER 4

The Second "C": Compatibility

So, you've had great sex with someone new for a couple weeks and now it's starting to slow down. As you start spending more *out-of-the-bedroom* time with them, you notice you might not be so compatible.

For example, football season just started and you now understand that they're a Chicago fan and you're a lifelong Green Bay fan. The sight of them in the opposing team's jersey sickens you and makes them less attractive. What's even more difficult is figuring out which section you're going to sit in when you attend the games together. We probably should not even talk about the ride home after one of your teams loses the game.

You are also starting to see that they go to the gym every day at 5 a.m. and you want to sleep in and work out at night or maybe not at all. However, they somehow insinuate that you are lazy. So, you forgo sleep to join them for a 5 a.m. workout, and you are secretly annoyed the whole time.

Perhaps they like to eat junk food and smoke marijuana. You haven't eaten fast food for over a decade and smoking anything sickens you.

Maybe you decide to go on a short trip together. However, they did zero planning, packed at the last minute, and barely made it to the airport on time. This left you feeling like you were their nagging parent through the entire ordeal.

Compatibility can be sexual too. For example, what if you notice that they haven't gone down on you since you started dating, and they finally tell you that they don't like to do that. What if that's a deal breaker for you? Why didn't they tell you this at the beginning so you could just pass and move on?

Perhaps they like anal. You're an "exit only" person. Maybe they like it fast, hard, and rough. You like it slow and sensual. Maybe they don't believe in monogamy; maybe you aren't the type that likes to share.

Sex can be as unique as the individual. So, it's not surprising that people can start to discover their new love interest's kinks and realize this is probably going to have to end.

You start spending more time in each other's homes. One morning, after you have mind-blowing sex, you offer to cook them breakfast. The entire time, they watch over your shoulder, freaking out about bacon grease splatters or questioning the way you decide to cook the eggs and toast. They finally just take over making breakfast, leaving you feeling inadequate and unappreciated. You were just trying to be nice, and they ruined the moment. To make matters worse, they seem oblivious to the fact that they have hurt your feelings.

To seal the deal, after breakfast, you clear the table and start putting dishes in the dishwasher. They come behind you and start taking them back out of the dishwasher to rinse them. They place them back in the dishwasher, but in a different way than you had originally. You can tell that they are disgusted with your method and they think you're a total mess. Why do they have to be so critical?

You go home disappointed because the sex was *so* good and they're *so* hot, but, in the end, you know this relationship isn't going to last. As you're driving, it dawns on you. You realize that, all this time, you were paying more attention to what *they* didn't like about *you*, instead of asking yourself what *you* don't like about *them*! Surely you didn't set out to find some hyper-critical, emotionally unavailable egomaniac that is never going to appreciate you.

You were just someone they used to fill up that *very tiny* gap in their life between work, the gym, and time with friends and family. They wanted relationship privileges without committing to you or making you a priority. What's worse is you allowed yourself to settle for that.

Now, maybe being a gap filler is ok, if you were just looking to get your gap filled. However, for the most part, people like to be a priority. Ever since your last encounter with them, they've suddenly become perpetually "busy." You don't believe this because they always have time when they are horny or lonely. You are also "busy" and yet always find time for people you're interested in.

At this point, you start to wish that you hadn't rushed into bed with this person. Moreover, you wished you hadn't continued seeing them just because the sex was so good. You enjoy having sex with them, but every time you're with them, it becomes increasingly more clear that they couldn't care less about you as a person. You were just a free escort in their life.

Everything was on their terms. You only saw each other when it was convenient for *them*. Your needs never factored into the equation. You ended up feeling hurt, angry, and used.

Now what do you do? You know the answer, but you drag it out and it starts to get ugly. *You* start to get ugly. You're mad at them and you're mad at *yourself*. You didn't have compatible relationship goals, but you emotionally invested anyway.

Are you getting the picture? Again, knowing yourself, embracing who you are and what you want is essential to getting out of these types of situations before you invest too much physically and emotionally.

What if you could have avoided it? What if you knew that you should've pumped the brakes a little sooner during the chemistry phase to assess other things? Could this have had a more positive outcome? I'm not advocating that you go through life avoiding every experience because they are messy, but sometimes the mess isn't worth the energy expended.

Some encounters can be messy but beautiful at the same time; and you'd choose to do it all over again, even though it didn't turn out the way you'd hoped. Perhaps you learned something valuable about yourself during some of those moments. Some experiences can help you figure out what you don't want in a relationship, and that's just as important as knowing what you do want.

The bottom line here is that being incompatible with someone causes anxiety, stress, and disrupts your peace. Is that really what you want out of your romantic connections? Whether your romantic connection is intended to be for fun or for longevity, isn't it also supposed to be positive and enjoyable? How can you enjoy yourself if the emotions this person predominantly brings out in you are annoyance, aggravation, hurt, insecurity, inadequacy, or anger?

Is that their fault? Weren't they just being themselves? Isn't that what we should all strive to do? Did they really do something wrong or were they just not compatible with you? Not wanting you in the same way that you wanted them, or wanting you more than you intended is not a crime. Are they really a nasty, insensitive scumbag or should you take responsibility for your own actions and contributions?

The point is, they didn't know you when you first met. They didn't know what you liked and what you disliked. It was your job to communicate those things. So, try to remember that when an encounter doesn't work out the way you hoped. If you're the one deciding to move on, accept responsibility for your decision to engage with this person and don't knock them for just being who they are. Try to leave the situation with empathy, gratitude, and grace.

Not every end has to be sad and hateful. Sometimes you can end a romantic relationship with someone but end up with a lifelong friend. I've had this happen several times in my life. This is certainly the case with the father of my children. We married very young, but I'd do it all over again even though it didn't work out romantically. He is a great co-parent, but more importantly, he is my dear friend.

One big reason that we were able to get to this place was due to the fact that we were *compatible* in wanting our kids to be happy. That shared value compelled us to set our differences aside time and time again. As the years passed, our relationship pain healed and our friendship solidified. We've had so many great family moments together. He's someone I couldn't imagine having lived life without.

Another reason things could end well could be due to the fact that you met at the wrong time. Bad timing. You may have both had an amazing time with each other, but your love interest is getting ready to take a new position in another state. It's a great opportunity for them and they've worked hard for it. Unfortunately, your life just doesn't allow for a long-distance relationship right now. You have small children at home and aging parents who rely heavily on you.

Your lifestyles are not compatible at this moment, but it doesn't take away from the great people that you both are. Instead of being angry with one another, you choose to be happy for the time you've shared. You even keep the door open for friendship. It was a truly wonderful experience and now you have a great example of what might work for you in the future.

Now, more often than not, it seems that peaceful, positive break-ups are not the norm. It depends on the reasons it ended and the actions of both parties. If you're dealing with cantankerous creatures that just can't see anything but their own pain and anger, it can get pretty toxic.

In these situations, it seems that no matter what you do or say, they always turn it into a big, emotional affair. Their version of the truth will never match yours. Reasoning with them is completely off the table. Trying to have a conversation with them is like talking to an enraged ape. You can't comfort them, and you certainly can't make them less angry. In fact, you're probably afraid to go near them. Who wouldn't be?

The good news here is that you're not responsible for someone else's inability to be a mature adult. Regulating one's emotions is something that each person has to do for themselves. So, if you find yourself trying to navigate the end of a relationship with someone who is a raging rhinoceros or a hysterical hyena, recognize that you are not the ringmaster in this circus. This person is grown and will have to process their feelings on their own.

All you can do is endeavor to have empathy and take responsibility for your contributions to the current scenario. In the end, you'll probably just need to close that door… or slam it. You might even consider bolting that thing shut and not looking back. Whew!

You do not have to stay in a vat of toxicity. You do not have to be an emotional beating post for someone who lacks basic coping skills. If you weren't sure about your incompatibility with this person before, it's probably becoming as clear as the sky on a cloud-free day in the tropics.

Also, don't look at areas of incompatibility and think you did something wrong. Worse yet, don't feel that you need to change. This just wasn't *your* person.

Change if *you* want to change, but you are probably just fine the way you are. Cherish the good memories but don't let this experience wreck your rainbow. Be conscious of not projecting this experience onto the next person you meet. Just use what you've learned to be more aware of who you are compatible with.

Being incompatible is just that. It's not evil. No one is wrong and no one is right. However, as you can see, being incompatible with someone can bring a lot of conflict into your relationships. I didn't realize this until I met someone that I was compatible with, and experienced how little we fought about things. We just seemed to flow.

Whenever we were deciding on an issue, we seemed to decide much quicker and always seemed to choose similar ways to handle issues. This was because we were totally comfortable being ourselves and *honest* with one another. We were particularly compatible about our views on family and raising children. Our relationship didn't work out, but we remain great friends to this day.

Up until this point, we've been talking about interactions with people who were purely incompatible. We have not addressed people who blatantly lied, misrepresented themselves, their relationship goals, their living arrangement status, or their fetish for penguins in bikinis. If someone intentionally fabricates an image of themselves to attract you into wanting them, there's little you can do until you uncover the truth. When you do figure it out, you'll probably be, understandably, angry.

I have to say that in my dating adventures, I've come across *so* many people who like to conceal the truth about themselves or tell me a story about the image of themselves that they want me to believe. They even have a great reason for why their past relationship didn't work out. No surprise;

it's usually not *their* fault. The same is true when you ask about their current situation.

I've found that most people like to paint themselves in a very positive light. They definitely don't want to highlight their ugly parts. They have a version of the truth that they find palatable to themselves, and they are firmly committed to it. In fact, they've told the story so many times that they don't even really believe or remember the actual truth anymore.

This new, manufactured truth has become fact in their minds. They tell this story to make themselves more attractive to others. It's how they want to see themselves and how they want others to see them. So, they withhold key facts and information to entice you into wanting them. The truth is just too hard for even them to handle. Misrepresenting yourself makes it even more difficult to find someone you're compatible with.

To demonstrate this point, let's say a man is homophobic. He's recently met a woman who he's incredibly physically attracted to. Soon after, he realizes this independent, badass woman has no less than fifty gay friends. He immediately knows that their views on key issues don't align. Specifically, she would be opposed to his stance on LGBTQ+ issues.

The problem is the homophobe thinks she is freaking hot, and just wants to have sex with her so badly. So, he hides his homophobia and makes excuses every time she asks him to go out with her gay friends. The sight of her friends being affectionate with one another makes him uncomfortable.

As the relationship progresses, he also fails to tell her about his antiquated stance on women's rights. He's grown tired of her *independence*. It makes him feel inadequate. He doesn't like that she's not easy to control. He knows this relationship can't last but keeps his true feelings hidden. The sex with her is *so* good. She also does his laundry, and meal preps for him *every week*!

So, he continues to act the part until he *gets* her to want him. Then, slowly, he starts to let down his guard and shield of dishonesty. One day, he snaps and goes on a tirade against one of these groups of people. His truth is revealed. The object of his desire has seen who he truly is and she's gone.

Hearts are broken. She's feeling hurt, angry, and lied to. Tires are getting slashed. Clothes are getting thrown out of windows; and *now* we have *all* the drama! Oh, how fun for you both.

How did he think this was going to end? Why wouldn't he want to spend his energy being more authentic so that he could find a more compatible partner?

He created a fictitious person for her to fall for—of course they're not compatible. The person she was developing feelings for didn't even exist!

One doesn't have to look far these days to see misrepresentations of the truth. Just look at social media and the plethora of filters people use on their photos to make themselves look good.

If you think filtered photos are something only women do, then, to my male audience, please ask your closest female friend or family member to check out any dating site from their perspective. It will take you less than five minutes to see it's not something just women do. Not only do men use filters, they also post photos from when they were a competitive bodybuilder twenty years ago.

After you've swiped on their filtered, photo-shopped ass, you arrange to go meet them; and walk right past them because you didn't even recognize them. They look nothing like the photos on their profile. In fact, their body is so much larger and softer than what was represented. You're so annoyed by this person's misrepresentations, you just turn around and leave. Block. Delete.

Another example is people who post images of themselves always being upbeat and projecting financial security. They're always doing something *fun* or interesting. Then once the camera is off, they're curled up on their couch, depressed and not showering for days. Every time they post something, they are careful not to capture the ants crawling across the dirty floor of their studio apartment, or the eviction notice stuck on the front door.

My personal favorites are those that never dress up, or wear a suit. Then, they're asked to stand up in their best friend's wedding, and for the next five years the only photos on their profile are the wedding photographer's. The thing is, they *hate* suits. They're only ever going to show up to a date wearing cargo shorts or workout clothes. In fact, they don't even own a suit; they rented that one for the wedding. So why not just show themselves in their natural state?

We all have friends and loved ones who we've watched post their fake images on social media. As their friends, we know they don't go to the gym early in the morning. In fact, they hardly ever go to the gym at all.

Who are they trying to be; and–wait, whose house are they in? Everyone knows their house isn't that clean. Where is this dog from? They don't even like animals. Why are they pretending to eat healthy? We all know they only like fast food. Who are they trying to impress? Has someone hacked their account?

It seems to be a prevalent thing these days. We've probably all posted photos of us looking like we are "living our best lives." The need to project an image, rather than our true selves, is one of the biggest reasons I wanted to write this book. I'm sick and tired of dating people's fictitious images!

Why are we wooing people with filtered photos and embellished versions of the truth? We all know it doesn't take long to find out the truth. Why are we telling fictional stories about ourselves, instead of reality? It's not going to take much to figure out that you're not really a bodybuilder when we meet and your pecs are now saggier than grandma's boobs.

This used to make me so angry. I felt like I wasn't given all the information that would allow me to make decisions that were best for *me*. I was strung along until I finally pieced things together and the truth was revealed. Then, I would try to have a conversation to get the entire truth.

That is so funny to me now. I wanted the truth from someone who couldn't even be honest with *themselves*! The truth is, they probably don't like who *they* see in the mirror, so they conceal those undesirable parts.

How about we all stop focusing on attracting the "*right*" person with our lies and stories? Instead, why don't we spend more time on becoming a real, authentic, and honest person? A person who knows what we like and what we don't like; and more importantly, is comfortable communicating those things. What if we take that approach and see what options are presented? Then, instead of going from the bedroom to the chapel, we are intentionally more selective about who we allow into our lives.

Wouldn't relationships be more enjoyable if we made a conscious effort to assess compatibility before investing further? In order to find someone you are compatible with, you need to be your *true authentic self*. You need to let others see and experience the real you. If you are faking your interest just so another person will find you compatible, how long will this house of cards stand? Probably about as long as a tent in a tornado.

If we overlook compatibility or falsely manipulate it, it can lead us to our third "C." The "C" that can often be the most revealing, yet is probably everyone's least favorite. Our next "C" is Conflict.

CHAPTER 5

The Third "C": Conflict

Conflicts arise in all relationships: whether romantic, platonic, or familial. We've all witnessed people handle conflict very differently. Some approaches are more effective than others.

For example, some people stop talking to their partner for weeks; while others spontaneously explode. Then, there are the mixed signal people, who smile while plotting something evil. Let's not forget about the over communicators who have verbal diarrhea and will talk the issue to death. We can all appreciate the real ones who recognize they did something they're not proud of and apologize. Or how about those that just walk away for good, with the mindset that it's just not worth talking or fighting over.

We can't overlook narcissists, who can't accept responsibility or apologize for their actions. Their egos wouldn't let us overlook them anyways. How do they always find a way to turn the conversation around, and make it about what *you* did wrong? Blaming *you* for the conflict, based on your reaction to *their* bad behavior.

Being aware of how you respond and react to conflict is a critical part of any relationship. Are you someone who contributes to the problem, or to the solution? Do you like to be the helpless victim, or the heroic knight? Are you a lion, roaring wildly to intimidate your target, or an ostrich burying your head in the sand? Can you be a partner, or are you a project?

Do you create conflict to see someone fight for you? Maybe you like all the passion and drama of conflict, not to mention the make-up sex.

Possibly, you like to avoid conflict at all costs. Instead, you opt for tolerating unbearable things you don't like just to stay with your current love interest. Perhaps you're the type that likes to talk things out for *hours,* constantly repeating yourself. You are unaware that you never allow your partner the opportunity to contribute to the conversation.

Whether you like to talk, fight, run, hide, cry, or hug it out, awareness is key. It is advisable to keep an open mind. Also, try to refrain from making sweeping generalizations and inferential leaps about the other person's intentions and actions until you hear their side. When they do tell you their side, actively listen to what they are saying, instead of focusing on formulating your responses and tuning them out.

Let's explore this in some examples.

You've been dating someone now for several months. Things are seemingly going great. The sex is fire. They watch football with you on the weekends; and never cheer for the opposing team. You both like to work out at night and eat cheat meals on Saturdays. You've never had a relationship go this well, and you're excited about the future with this person.

Recently, your boss asked for someone to step up and take on a new project at work. You volunteered and now have less time to spend with your love interest. This weekend, you had to back out of an event because you needed to work in order to meet these new deadlines.

When you tried to explain your situation, the conversation ended with your love interest accusing you of being selfish, not caring about them, and losing interest in them. They accuse you of lying about work and suggest that you are using it as an excuse to spend time with someone else and then they hang up on you. Now they are ignoring your texts and phone calls, and you have no idea what just happened. You think they are acting unstable and immature, so you send them an explosive text to let them know just how immature they are.

> You: I can't believe you're accusing me of fucking someone else. When would I have the time? When I'm not working, I have to spend all of my time with you because you're such an attention seeking whore. You're so insecure. Grow the fuck up! I'm not your ex. Get some counseling.

Now you're both sitting there waiting for the other person to "act right" and apologize.

What does that mean exactly, to "act right"? And what are you each apologizing for? Who sets the expectations and standards for "acting right"? What if no one was wrong? What if you both just lacked empathy, understanding, and mind reading abilities?

What if you both lacked conflict resolution skills? Let's analyze this a little more.

Looking at it from the perspective of the person who has been ditched, your love interest has just backed out of a super important event. You are being recognized for something you've been working toward for several years now. Furthermore, all your friends and family will be there; and you planned to introduce your new love interest to them.

To make matters worse, your prior love interest would always back out of things last minute saying it was "work-related." However, you found out they were seeing other people behind your back. When confronted, your ex would gaslight you, turning the situation around and somehow making *you* the reason they felt compelled to cheat and lie.

All these experiences start flooding your thoughts. You are now officially triggered. You're reliving old wounds and projecting those onto your new love interest.

You can't believe that your new love interest isn't going to be with you on this important evening. You are crushed and feel like you are not a priority in their life. You feel like you completely misjudged them and their interest in you. You are fully convinced that they are seeing other people and this "work thing" is just an excuse.

In response to this story you're telling yourself, because that's what this is, a story (and an unsubstantiated one at that), your reaction follows. The first thing you do in response to this story, that you are now fully committed to, is start making assumptions about their character. You find yourself coming to conclusions about how lowly you rank in their life and you proceed to cut them off.

You block them on your phone and all social media, based on the actions of a completely different person from your past. Your current partner has been nothing but caring and consistent with you, but somehow you have vilified them into being *just like your ex*.

On the other side of this equation, the person who has backed out of the event is feeling completely confused and hurt by your reactions. Since meeting you, they've never been happier. You've inspired them to work harder, be more responsible, and get their finances in order. They thought you were such a badass and felt like they needed to work harder to come up to your level.

So, when their boss asked for someone to step up and take on this assignment, they volunteered. They wanted to be a better version of themselves to show you that they are a *worthy*, long-term relationship candidate for you. Being successful in this new assignment will mean a promotion, more money, and better positioning to provide for a family in the future. A family they can see starting with *you*.

They thought you'd be proud of them and that you'd admire their work ethic. They were excited about the chance of getting a promotion and being a better provider in the future. This was something their prior love interest said they would never achieve.

You inspired them to work harder, to be more financially stable, and they were happy to change because they wanted you to be proud. They also did this because they could see a future with, you guessed it, *you*!

When you accused them of cheating and not caring, it hurt them. It made them question everything about the relationship. Then, there was the silent treatment; a deal-breaker for them. Their ex *always* did that to manipulate the situation and get what they wanted.

Their ex would shut them out until they were at a breaking point. Then, when they couldn't bear it any longer, they would just give in. Nothing would get resolved in their prior relationship, and the pattern would repeat. It led to great unhappiness in their personal life and the relationship. They felt they didn't matter and that their pain was never considered. They vowed *never* to date someone who uses that tactic *ever* again. It's toxic, manipulative, and abusive.

To ensure your conflict drags out as long as possible, you both share your versions of the truth and frustration with your inner circles. To no one's surprise, your inner circles agree with their respective parties based on only the facts provided.

This validates your respective conclusions and your decisions to continue to act the way you both are acting. The result? You both continue on your path and wait for the other person to acknowledge how wrong they were.

Does anyone else see the train wreck that is occurring? What is the right way to handle conflict?

By now you should know I don't have the answer to that question; and this book will not tell you the right or wrong way to deal with conflict. This book is about getting *you* to think about how *you* deal with conflict. Knowing that can help you respond differently. It can help you contribute to the solution, instead of perpetuating the conflict.

Let's continue with an alternate version of our scenario. What if the person who got the new work assignment told their love interest what it represented as soon as they accepted it? What if they told their love interest they were inspired to do this because they saw a future with them, and wanted to be a great provider? What if they shared that their ex doubted them, and it has bothered them for years?

Alternatively, what if the person being stood up shared how important this event was to them; that all their friends and family would be there? What if this person shared that their ex had frequently cheated on them, using work as a cover? Imagine how different the outcome could be if each party didn't jump to conclusions based upon their own internal narratives.

The point is to own up to your shortcomings about how you might be perpetuating conflicts. In this scenario, both parties didn't take any time to let the real facts and circumstances unfold. Nor did they seek out the truth from each other. They just imposed their past onto the situation and let it dictate their actions.

We have all encountered individuals that can never be reasoned with. For whatever reason, be it insecurity, narcissism, anger issues, learned helplessness, pride, or ego, some people are just committed to perpetuating their narrative. If you even attempt to point out real facts or hold them accountable for their actions, the conflict escalates.

Now, I could literally write a whole chapter on each one of these things, but I'm not going to do that. I'm simply trying to highlight awareness of people who are committed to contributing to the conflict, and not the resolution. You cannot change them, reason with them, or make them feel remorse.

As mentioned in the previous chapter, you only have control over what *you* do. They probably are not going to be honest with you about these traits anyway. I mean, how many dating profiles have you encountered where a person has written, "Hi. I'm Brian. I'm a narcissistic, gaslighting asshole"?

Maybe that just set off a lightbulb, and you're able to match that statement with a person in your life who fits this description. No matter how hard you try to resolve the conflict or focus on a resolution, this person just keeps rehashing it. They make it their life's mission to constantly find new things to fight about. They're certainly never going to accept any ownership of the conflicts they contribute to.

They would also never give a real apology. The best you might get is an "I'm sorry you feel that way."

This is a cop out. Run! Don't walk! Far away!

This says you're the problem because of how *you're* processing *their* actions. It doesn't acknowledge how *their actions* made *you* feel; nor is there any hope this person will be mindful of that in the future. They're certainly not going to join in your attempts at conflict resolution. The only villain, in their story, is *you*.

Maybe *you* are this person? If you are, you're probably not going to acknowledge it. You've told yourself too many stories about how everyone else is to blame. Forget that you seem to be having the same experiences with different people over and over again. You are a master of vilifying others and remaining the helpless, blameless victim. Poor you.

Again, this book isn't going to help you with that. You wouldn't acknowledge that you need help anyway. Just keep telling yourself you're a victim. You get more sympathy that way. Even better, by not taking ownership of your shitty behavior, you *never* have to change.

In fact, you start all your relationships off by telling your love interests all about the horrible things that have been *done to you* by others. You're perpetually blameless. The thing is, though, your relationships only last as long as it takes the new person to figure out these *horrible things* that were *done to you*, were not an accurate representation of the facts and circumstances.

Why? Well, they've only been with you for two weeks, and already figured out the story you told them about your exes never spending time with you seems suspicious. Since they started dating you, they've seen you have no money to pay your bills, but you begged them to take multiple "sick" days with you because you want attention. In fact, they're starting to think your need for attention is insatiable.

Guess what happens next? If you guessed that you are going to have the same conflict and argument with yet another love interest, you are correct!

Another thing that makes me run away faster than you can say "manipulator," is when someone gives me the silent treatment. It screams, "Hey! I have zero conflict resolution skills! I'm just going to sit over here like a giant, pouty toddler until you break!"

This can also look like "ghosting," a new phenomenon where a person figuratively drops off the face of the earth, never to be heard from again. This can happen when a conflict ensues. It's an avoidance technique. They would rather stop talking to you and seeing you, than resolve an issue or admit their wrongdoing.

After a while, could be weeks or months, they start feeling lonely or horny. Then, out of the blue, *ding!*, they text you.

"Hey Baby! I was just thinking about you. What's good?"

This is "zombieing." It is also a new element to dating. Zombieing occurs when someone has ghosted you, acting as if they're dead, then all of a sudden, POOF! They're back! Just like a zombie.

When people conduct themselves like this, they are intentionally putting the conflict on a timeout. It's another avoidance tactic. They ghosted (checked out of the conflict) because they didn't want to apologize for their behavior, nor did they want to accept any accountability for their actions.

They hoped you'd forget about it, maybe even miss them, because they are *so* fabulous.

Now, weeks or months later, they're drunk, lonely, and horny, scrolling through their phone to revisit their options. Guess who they decided should scratch their itch? Yep, *you*. Aren't you the lucky one! They needed that ego boost, that magic pussy, or big dick energy you brought to the table, so they broke down and texted you.

You're now left staring at your phone, thinking, "What in the actual hell is wrong with this person?!" You might even be tempted to respond. Just know that if you respond with anything other than "Hey boo. I missed you so much," they're just going to ghost you again. They aren't interested in acknowledging their behavior. They are also, most certainly, not going to engage in a conversation that holds them accountable.

This person is showing you something important about their character. Pay attention! Sure, they might be sexy and can suck a golf ball through a hose or write their name in cursive with their tongue, but look past chemistry. This is an opportunity to assess their other C's like communication, conflict, and choices before jumping back into bed with them.

This person is showing you how *every* conflict with them will be handled. They're showing you that they have zero conflict resolution skills. They're also showing you that they are manipulative. They're showing you the choices they would rather make like ghosting and avoiding accountability for their actions.

Another prevalent phenomenon, and conflict resolution train wreck, is a term called "gaslighting." This term is derived from Patrick Hamilton's 1938 play *Gas Light*. It refers to a psychological manipulation where one person makes another doubt their own perceptions or reality.

This creates confusion, not solutions. Let me give you an example.

Imagine you're with your boo looking forward to a great evening at home. You're snuggled up, watching your favorite crime show, and they're "working" on their laptop. In actuality, though, they are chatting with their "lover!" The two of them are trying to figure out how your partner is going to get out of spending time with you tonight.

You try to kiss them and see that they are texting a woman that they have previously claimed is "just a friend." You catch a glance at the texts and they are 100% flirtatious and romantic in nature.

Your partner immediately becomes protective of their computer screen and starts accusing you of invading their privacy. They also tell you that you're imagining things. You know what you saw but they are telling you that you are crazy and can't read.

When you ask to see the text messages, they escalate the situation into a full-fledged argument. Now they are headed into their closet to get dressed. While trying to find something to wear, they act mad about you trying to look at their computer. You explain that you were just trying to kiss them, but then saw the flirty messages. They tell you that you are hallucinating and they are tired of your insecurity. They storm out of the house and you are left at the front door wondering what the hell just happened?

In their haste, they didn't close their laptop or log out of their messages app. As you are standing there, you see a message that was just sent to your boo from their "friend" that says, "Hurry, I can't wait to feel you inside of me." What's worse is the message is from a married woman and your boo had recently introduced you to her *and* her *husband*!

They've become your new couple friends. He even brought them over on Valentine's Day to have dinner with you both. You were upset by this because you wanted to spend the day alone, just the two of you; but your boo insisted they come.

Now you're remembering how this woman became very upset every time he showed affection toward you. She even stormed out of the room once. You were concerned about her so you went to check on her to see if she was ok. She told you that it was just hard to watch you and your boo be affectionate with one another because her husband is not that way with her. You hugged her and attempted to comfort her!

You recall previously trying to talk to your boo about the weird vibe and flirting you observed between them. However, he repeated his behavior of getting mad at you and calling you insecure. In fact, this has happened several times to the point where you were starting to doubt your own recollection. You even started to think that you might be insecure.

Tonight, however, it hits you like a brick. She wasn't upset with her husband, she was upset seeing your boo be affectionate with *you* because *she* wanted his attention. Right in your own home!

All of your emotions come to the forefront.

You've been looking after his kids while he "worked weekends," and have been paying all the bills. You knew something wasn't adding up, literally, because all that overtime he was putting in sure as hell wasn't translating into more money on his paycheck! Every time you questioned the discrepancy between the hours he worked and the money he was taking home, he said you were nuts.

You've been holding down everything to help him get on his feet and now you find out that he wasn't trying to be on his feet. He was trying to be on his knees balls deep inside this bitch.

You pull out your phone and take a photo of the messages and send it to both of them in a group text. Ten minutes later guess who's back at the house? Yep, your man. The best part is he's not apologetic at all. In fact, he's furious with *you*!

He's going on and on, trying to make this situation all about you looking at his private messages. He screams, "How dare you look through my messages? This shit is private! What's the matter with you? Doesn't my privacy mean anything to you?"

You are beyond confused. You must have missed something. Did he forget the messages that you just read because he left his computer right there on the bed? Did he forget that he was the one who couldn't get out of the door fast enough to meet his lover? Is he really blaming this all on you?

The answer is yes. His goal was to put you on the defensive and redirect the conflict that *he* created.

Let's say he is successful in making it all about you instead of his cheating ass. In the days that follow, he gives you the silent treatment. He never acknowledges how hurt you must be at finding out he was cheating on you. Instead, he just keeps the conflict fixated on you invading his privacy by reading his messages with his lover.

This goes on for days. Then, somehow, you're not even sure how, you're begging him to talk to you and to forgive *you* for looking at his computer. What? How did that happen?

Congratulations! You just showed him how easy it is to cheat on you and take advantage of you emotionally, physically, and financially. Is this really the person you are so in love with?

What exactly is keeping you here?

What brought you two together?

What if this person had told you on your first date they were a lying, cheating, insecure player?

What if they told you they needed you to financially support them and their kids while they went out and fucked other people that they found more physically attractive than you? Would you have said, "Oh how great! You are everything that I've been looking for! I can't wait to be treated like shit by you!"

What if you are this person? Would you ever be honest with a person about the fact that you are only using them for money, security, and free childcare? Would you even be honest with yourself about how desperate you are for financial security? How many times have you passed up a really great person because they didn't have the money you needed to sustain the lifestyle you wanted for yourself?

Let's look at another scenario. You and your partner always fight about money. They never seem to have any and you always end up having to cover the essentials like rent, food, car payments, car insurance, etc. Every month the bills are generally the same amount and come out at the same time but your partner can never seem to get them paid. It's always a last-minute conversation, too.

You're angry because you give them money to cover the bills but always end up having to pay out more money because your partner doesn't pay them. You know they are using your money to fund their lifestyle instead of using it to pay bills.

This month, it happened again. When the Amazon packages arrived at the doorstep, you asked them if this was going to create any issues with paying the bills this month.

They got furious with you and told you to stop acting like you're their parent instead of their partner. They tell you they already paid some of the bills for the month.

For the next two days they barely talk to you and when they do it's only to mock you. Just this morning, while you were eating breakfast, they asked you if eating that bougie avocado would impair your ability to pay your bills.

A week later, you notice they are wearing a new outfit and a brand new pair of designer shoes. You don't want to bring it up, but you know they barely earn enough to cover their bills. You know they don't have room in their budget for this type of purchase. You've gone over it time and time again. Their monthly earnings barely cover necessities. You are, again, concerned that this month's bills are going to fall on your shoulders.

Rather than complimenting them on their new outfit, you ask them how they are going to pay their car payment and insurance. As expected, they lose their shit. They tell you that you're not their parent, and even if you were, they don't need your commentary.

They swear that they have everything covered. They tell you that if you loved them, you wouldn't be treating them like this. They tell you that you don't care about them and that you just can't stand to see them looking good. You're clearly just jealous.

Another few weeks pass. You happen to come home early from work because there was a power outage and so your boss sent you home. You rarely get home this early and you are looking forward to the extra hours of personal time. You decide to stop and get the mail on your way to your apartment. You rarely get the mail because you always get home after your partner, who usually collects it.

You open the mailbox and you see three envelopes. Each one bears big red stamps and stickers that read, "URGENT," "PAST DUE," and "REQUIRES IMMEDIATE ATTENTION." One is from the financial institution where they pay their car loan. Another is from the electric company. The last one is from your property management company.

You open the ones that also have your name on them and it confirms what you already suspected to be true. The bills are not being paid. As you walk up to the door of your apartment, you see an eviction notice stuck on the door. Your stomach sinks.

You enter the apartment and see your partner standing there opening more Amazon packages. You take the eviction notice and place it on the kitchen counter with the past due notices. You say nothing. Your facial expressions say it all. There's no way that they can deny it now, you're holding the proof.

Just when you thought it couldn't get any worse, they speak. The response is utterly insane. Your partner tells you that there must be a mistake. They tell you that they saw the money come out of their account. When you ask to see their bank statements, they lose their mind. Now they are slamming things on the counter, accusing you of not having their back. Telling you that you should trust them.

You're stunned. You simply can't believe what you are hearing.

You're holding the proof of what you've been concerned about in your own hands, yet they are in full denial. Their only response is to attack your character. You know that this relationship has come to its end.

The only thing you can do now is save yourself any further heartache and torture. You quietly walk to your bedroom and start packing up your belongings. There's no point in trying to reason with them. Past arguments have shown you there is no resolution because they will never admit they are the reason for this conflict.

While you pack, your partner is in the kitchen continuing their attacks on your character. You put your earbuds in and drown out the sounds with some music. A better life is on the other side of all this packing.

Maybe you are the other person in this example. Do you find yourself having the same conflict over and over again, but with different people? Is there a common theme? If so, maybe it's time to be honest with *yourself*.

Again, you are who you are. That's what this book is all about. You can lie about it, or try to conceal it, but eventually the truth always has a way of surfacing. Maybe you're not willing to accept that these characteristics exist in you. But if you can't accept these characteristics in yourself, then how do you expect others to? Are you so wrapped up in the image you need to present to the world, you can't face or accept your truth?

Lying about who you are does nothing but create conflicts. Withholding facts, circumstances, and concealing information is manipulative. So often, with conflict, we might think to ourselves, "My love interest knows I'm *like this,"* or, "*They know what I mean.*"

That is an assumption. While they might know that you are a certain way, they'd like you to be different. Is *your way* causing conflict? More importantly, do you want to be different?

If the answer is no, then you're back to the chapter on compatibility.

If you find yourself constantly frustrated with someone's conflict resolution skills or lack thereof, they may not be the person for you. Sure, the sex was fire; but outside of the bedroom, you are in constant conflict with this person.

So now what? This is another aspect of yourself that you have to get closely acquainted with. How long will you try to fit this square peg in your round hole? Pun intended.

Are you starting to see the value in establishing a vetting process that evaluates more than just chemistry? How many weeks, months, or years are you willing to waste in constant conflict with someone whose communication style irritates you? If you are trying to find a relationship that enhances your life, protects your peace, and produces more joy than anxiety, you're probably starting to realize that knowing yourself in these areas helps you evaluate and navigate these traits in others.

Another way of looking at it is if you know you are baking soda, then you also know that vinegar is always going to make you have an explosive reaction. So, why do you keep trying to get into relationships with vinegar?

Conversely speaking, maybe you are chocolate and you know that you work extremely well with peanut butter. In fact, you become a better version of yourself when you mix yourself up with peanut butter. Don't you want your interaction with your love interest to be like chocolate and peanut butter instead of an explosive, horribly tasting, voluminous mass of foam?

Know yourself. Accept yourself. Be conscious about what causes you to erupt and also how your own characteristics trigger others. Be honest about what you can and cannot change about yourself. The person you've been dating may be a great person, just not the person for you. With you, its never-ending conflict. You're tired of constantly trying to find solutions to these topics of contention. You don't mind talking, but you want to talk about more enjoyable things.

Be honest with yourself and know when to walk away. Also be brave about realizing and acknowledging when the person perpetuating the problem is none other than *yourself*. The sooner you own that shit and are aware of how you're contributing to the problem, the sooner you can start creating the solution.

Alternatively, you might be that person who goes into an argument just to *win*. What are you winning exactly? Asshole of the Year Award?

If you're the person arguing with an asshole, sometimes you just have to accept that the only resolution in some relationships is *dissolution*, meaning you dissolve the relationship. You choose to walk away from this person because their ugliness isn't something you're willing to tolerate.

Whew! Conflict is *stressful!*

Once you get through the first big fight with your boo, you've probably learned a lot about yourself, and them. You might have gained some awareness about your triggers and respective boundaries. You potentially even learned some additional things about people you're more compatible with.

One major contributor to conflict which needs to be discussed is Communication. Conflict and communication definitely go together, and can significantly impact one another.

Bad communication can start a conflict, while good communication can neutralize it. Bad communication can fuel a conflict to the point of no communication. Good communication can bring two people back from a problem they never thought they'd resolve.

Communication is a game changer, or a conflict changer, if you will. Whether we change the conflict for *better* or for *worse* depends heavily on your communication skills. So, let's talk about it.

To our next C: Communication.

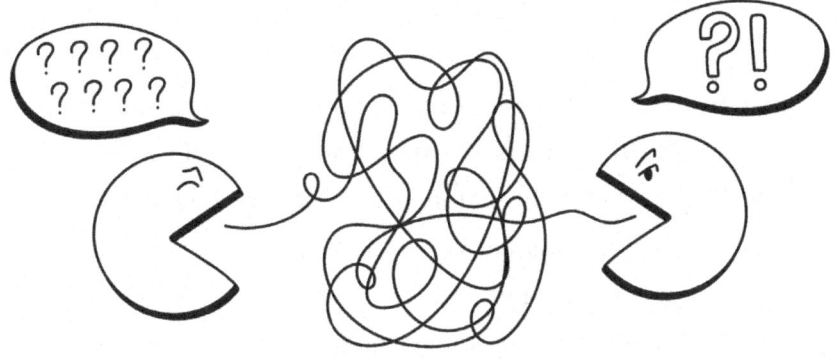

CHAPTER 6

The Fourth "C": Communication

Communication can be verbal or non-verbal. It can be conveyed in our body language, our actions, the tone of our voice, and the look on our face; or through the shade of purple you turn during an argument.

Perhaps you just got into a fight with your boo, and now they come into the kitchen, proceeding to slam all the cupboards while you are eating your dinner. They are letting you know just how they feel, yet they haven't said a word. However, if door slamming was a language, then you know that you have clearly just been called a motherfucker.

Alternatively, they could have walked into the kitchen, dropped to their knees, crawled under the table, and started giving you oral sex. Both of these methods of communication are non-verbal. One is obviously more enjoyable. Neither is really going to resolve your issues, however, the latter will probably alleviate your anxiety and stress.

On the other hand, maybe you and your partner have been frequently fighting about keeping the house clean and the fact that you do all the cooking. You're at your wits end and talking doesn't seem to do anything. You're so frustrated with your partner. The two of you haven't spoken in two days. You've even been sleeping in separate rooms. Is there any point to talking about it anymore? You've concluded that they don't care about what you said.

It's now the weekend and you're still lying in bed. You've been delaying getting up because you just can't take one more day of this. Finally, you pull yourself together, drag yourself out of bed and into the kitchen ready to clean up the mess your family has left there for you. You feel defeated before you even start your day.

As you open the door, bracing yourself for the war zone you are about to enter, you see your partner standing at the kitchen sink, doing the dishes! There are fresh lemon blueberry muffins on the counter, your favorite, and *coffee*! The floors have been mopped and every room is tidy. You can hear the washing machine in the background. You can't believe what you're seeing! The smell of fabric softener fills the air and you're *seriously* turned on. Who knew fabric softener was an aphrodisiac. Maybe you've just uncovered a new fetish.

That's when it hits you… you were actually *heard*. Your feelings mattered. No more words had to be spoken. Their actions are speaking now, and you've never felt more loved and cared about. As you walk towards your partner, they turn and see your tears. They wrap their arms around you and all the tension washes away.

Saturday mornings become something you look forward to, and it doesn't stop there. Your partner has created a schedule that splits the workload at home, and they've stuck to it. They heard you and have worked hard to show you, through their actions, that your feelings matter. They showed up for you and continue to show up. They contributed to the solution, not the conflict, and it feels good. Their actions were enough conversation.

Communication is also present in your tone and the facial expressions you use. How many memes have you seen of a woman saying, "I'm fine," in the most monotone unenthusiastic manner. Now add the fact her lips are barely moving and her teeth are clenched together. Is she really fine? Probably not. It's more likely she really wants to take all her man's most prized possessions and throw them in a dumpster filled with vomit.

How did he know she was angry when she clearly said she was "fine"?

Her tone.

He knows what she's like. He knows when she is happy. Right now, her tone is giving off more serial killer vibes than happiness. Now what? How should he approach the situation and get her to talk about what is bothering her? More importantly, why did she say she was fine when she clearly isn't?

Why can't people just say what they mean? How would you handle the situation? Would you leave because you don't really care to deal with it? Would you give them a hug? Would you go to Starbucks and bring back their favorite drink? What is your method of communication?

Imagine a woman asking her husband if he wants to go to the opera for their anniversary, which also happens to fall on Super Bowl Sunday. His own team is going to be in the game. When he doesn't respond the first three times she mentions it, she finally loses her patience and loudly asks, "Do you want to go or not?"

He yells back, face turning purple and the veins on the side of his head popping out, "YES! *FINE!* I'll go!"

Do you think she can tell he really doesn't want to do that on their anniversary?

Why didn't he say, "Babe, I know it's our anniversary this Sunday but it's also Super Bowl Sunday. I know you don't like football, but I really want to see this game. Can we go to the opera on Saturday? We can get box seats and even go to that fancy new restaurant you've been wanting to try. We can get a hotel room and ask my mom to watch the kids; make it a whole great night."

Wouldn't communicating have helped them both get what they wanted? As it stands now, how do you think their anniversary celebration is going to go? Talking it through, while difficult, could've made it much better for both of them.

Maybe your preferred method of communication is sarcasm. You say the opposite of everything you mean with a huge smirk. Suppose you've worked a lot of hours this week and you're just exhausted. This coming weekend you're looking forward to doing absolutely *nothing*. You don't even want to leave the house or talk to anyone. Your new love interest has been texting you all day wanting to plan a date, but you haven't responded. You just don't have any energy.

They've been asking all day if you want to go to the new Korean barbeque place. Great. On top of wanting to go out, they want you to go eat kimchi, the one food that gives you explosive diarrhea. Rather than communicating how you truly feel, you text "Oh yeah, that sounds great. I totally love it when my ass blows up from eating kimchi. It's really the best feeling in the world. Almost orgasmic."

Now, imagine you just started dating this person and they do not really know your sense of humor that well yet. It's also a text so they cannot hear the sarcasm in your voice. They receive the message and think to themselves, "Holy shit! What have I gotten myself into? Is this one of those pooping fetish people? Yeah, I'm out."

Perhaps you're the person who makes a joke out of every scenario. Like that one time when you were at your significant other's Aunt Betty's funeral for moral support.

You could see how upset they were and you really wanted everyone to lighten up. You also wanted, more than anything, to stay home because funerals make you anxious. However, you knew if you didn't go, you'd never hear the end of it.

So, you dragged yourself into the shower, put on something appropriate, and went off to look at ol' Aunt Betty. Truth was, she really didn't look much different. Aunt Betty always looked kind of dead when she was sleeping on the couch.

You arrived at the funeral home and you started to feel nauseous and sweaty just walking up to the place. Everyone was somewhat somber, but trying to be uplifting as Aunt Betty was eighty-eight years old and lived a good life. You were happy to join in the uplifting spirit, lighten the mood, and maybe even alleviate some of your own anxiety.

You made your way to the coffin to pay your respects, and just as you expected, Aunt Betty looked as old and dead as she normally did. So, with a big grin you said, "Well, she doesn't look any different now, does she? Maybe Aunt Betty was a zombie all these years. She looks like she could just jump right on out of that thing. Don't put your hip out Aunt Betty!"

You turned to your significant other while laughing and elbowing them, waiting for them to laugh at your jokes; but the look on their face was pure dread. They were mortified.

You only lived ten minutes from the funeral home but the drive home felt like two hours. Why couldn't you have just communicated how you felt? You're left hoping this will all blow over quickly. After all, your boo must know by now that you don't like funerals, right?

This might come as a big surprise, but most people are not psychic. I feel we often forget this, especially if we've been with someone for a long time. We start to assume that they *know* us and what we are thinking or feeling. While our inner circle may have a better handle at reading our moods than a complete stranger, it doesn't absolve us from clear communication. What if they get it wrong?

For example, what if you just ate poutine (a seriously high fat, French Canadian, culinary delight made of French fries, beef gravy, and cheese curds) and now your stomach is off. In fact, your stomach cramps are causing you to scowl and become generally cranky. What if this is right after your love interest said they wanted to talk to you about something important?

Historically, you have become cranky when you have to "talk." So now, your loved one thinks you are just shutting down, and becoming irritable to get out of talking. They start accusing you of that and you're wishing that you weren't so embarrassed about telling them you have to poop.

Let's explore another example.

Imagine, you have met someone wonderful when you weren't quite ready to be in a relationship? You were just

THE 7 C'S OF SELECTION | 81

looking for companionship and great sex. The thing is, though, you've always been a relationship person. You're used to being a priority in someone's life, not a casual love interest. Unfortunately, right now, you need to process your emotions about your most recent break up. You're lonely, horny, and your ego needs a boost. So, you go on a dating site to shop for viable candidates to fill all those voids.

You need to understand: you are looking for something casual. Therefore, *you* will *also* be something casual for the other person. You will not get boyfriend or girlfriend privileges. So, don't expect those benefits, or get mad when they treat you like the option that you are.

Let's say you meet someone and they spend the night. The next morning you want them to cook breakfast and help you move some boxes around in your garage. Basically, things that they would do for someone they're committed to. You want relationship privileges but you don't want to commit or invest anything into this situationship.

A couple of months have passed. You continue to spend time with each other. They are an extraordinary lover and you really enjoy your time together. You look forward to hearing from them. You've treated them very well. They, in turn, are very attentive to you, but only when you spend time together. When you are not together, you rarely hear from them.

Your mind wanders and you assume they are having sex with other people when they're not with you. It's really starting to bother you and make you sad. You want to be their priority. You don't want to admit it, but you've developed feelings for this person. You don't want to tell them, though, because you're afraid they will not feel the same. Besides, they should *know* how you feel. You've hinted at it before.

Last week, when you needed help doing some home improvements, they were non-committal and generally vague about their availability. You ended up mad, because if they cared about you, they should rush to help you with these things. You think to yourself, "That's it! This person is treating me like an option. I'm done."

You start taking longer to respond to their text messages and when you do respond, your messages are intentionally short and indifferent. You start to withdraw; increasing the dates you are going on with other people. You're sad, but you keep telling yourself that it's their fault. They didn't make you a priority.

At no point do you ever remind yourself that the other person doesn't know you've developed feelings. They are just going off of what you initially represented to them. The main part of these representations being that you were newly out of a relationship, and didn't want anything too serious. You were enjoying your freedom. So, they acted accordingly. They were giving you the space you initially asked for.

Now, they're wondering what is going on because they notice that you are withdrawing. Is it because you have drawn closer together? Has that scared you? Are you pulling away because you are not ready for a relationship yet? They are also sort of upset and sad; they thought that the two of you made a great couple.

Neither of you are great communicators.

You frequently cry through conversations when emotions are involved. They would prefer to avoid serious conversations. You're not willing to let them go yet, though; so, you tell yourself that you'll just slowly "unlove" them until you can pull away entirely.

You'd rather do this than have a conversation because you can't take any more rejection. They also fill a void in your life that you don't have anyone else lined up to fill. So, you decide not to voice your concerns. You'd rather just keep telling yourself your story.

What if it could be different, though?

What if you were brave enough to have the conversation with each other, and it turned out that you both had feelings for one another? It's definitely better than assuming that you are just an option to them and vice versa.

Of course, there is a risk that you could have the conversation and they say that they appreciate how you feel, but don't feel the same way. While that would probably hurt and wouldn't be what you were hoping, isn't it better to know the truth? Knowing the truth would allow you to make better decisions about who you should spend your time with. This information would allow you to move on and start investing in someone better suited for you.

Knowing your communication style can help you take responsibility in your relationships. Are you someone that shows extreme emotion, whether it be crying or raising your voice when trying to discuss and resolve something with your love interest? If you are, you need to understand that you are making the conversation more about your reaction than your message.

The person on the other side of your tears or anger isn't going to feel like you're creating a safe place for them to share their true feelings and opinions. A more likely outcome is they'll withdraw from the conversation, or withhold their true feelings because your emotions are taking center stage.

You've now put them in a position where they need to pacify you, instead of being honest. At some point, their true feelings will finally be revealed, and you'll probably ask them why they didn't tell you sooner. You will likely not take responsibility for letting your emotions derail the conversations, and the outcome, either.

Perfecting your communication skills isn't just important—it's your key to cutting through the bullshit and getting real with potential partners. Embrace the challenge and keep refining your approach. After all, the worst that can happen is losing someone who was never a good fit anyway. So, be bold and say it.

Now, on some off chance that you have miraculously used your communication skills to successfully navigate a big issue with your boo, you might be feeling confident in taking the next step. You're ready to introduce them to your friends and family, or as I like to refer to them–your *Community*.

Chemistry, compatibility, conflict, and communication are significantly influenced by our community. These are people who have been in our lives a long time, earned our trust, and often know us better than we know ourselves. They can be our trusted advisors, good examples of what we aspire to be, or they can be examples of how not to be.

Regardless of where your tribe falls on this continuum, we all have a community, even if it's our pets. So, let's explore that next.

Aren't you glad you get to come out from under the magnifying glass to dissect your inner circle?

CHAPTER 7

The Fifth "C": Community

Congratulations! You got through your first fight and finally stopped banging each other long enough to start being social again. You've had at least forty orgasms in the past couple weeks, and your oxytocin is at an all-time high; so it seems *logical* that you are now ready to take the next step with this person.

Surely, between all those orgasms, naps, and Netflix sessions, you've had a lot of meaningful conversations to get to know one another, right? Just look at the massive amount of thought you've put into this decision. Anyone who can give you forty orgasms in two weeks is alright in your books!

You're ready to introduce your love interest to your friends and family. After all, your body parts really like each other. What more do you need?

Surely your inner circle will see what you like about this person, right? Forget that *they* haven't been the ones having sex with your new love interest. Who cares that they will probably ask all the questions *you* should've been asking. What could go wrong? As it turns out… a lot!

Ah, our good ol' Community. Our friends who have been there for us through so many things we didn't even tell our own parents. The people that know all of our good parts *and* all of our ugly parts. How can anyone compare?

They've been with us through thick and thin. Always ready to lend an ear or give us advice. Oh, how we love that advice! Our precious community is always looking out for our best interests.

Alternatively, maybe your community is none of these things. It could be you come from a completely dysfunctional family and your definition of *friends* equates to party companions. After years of being a loner, and not really investing in relationships, your real community consists only of your two cats.

However you define your inner circle, that is what we are talking about in this chapter. So, here we go!

You're bringing your new romantic interest around your tribe. Great! Instant judgment seems like a spectacular relationship enhancer. Who are you going to start with? Your pets, friends, coworkers, siblings; or are you going straight for the parents? Let's walk through some scenarios.

You and your mom are super close and you happen to be having lunch today. You don't want to leave your new romantic interest alone in your apartment because you don't want them to go home yet. You've been enjoying *spending time together*. So, you invite them to *lunch with Mom*.

Your mom is the best! Does she have some quirks? Sure, she can sometimes (or frequently) be judgmental and condescending. Her interrogation techniques are fierce. She has also tried to insert her opinions and preferences in your romantic life many times. In all honesty, though, she doesn't really have a lot of standards; just that you date the person she selects.

Walking up to the restaurant you recall how, over the years, your mom has frowned upon everyone you've ever brought around. She thinks they're never good enough for you. She has also tried, relentlessly, to set you up with her friend's daughter, from the casino. The one with the *private subscription only* social media page, with hundreds of thousands of subscribers. When you mentioned this to your mom, she optimistically pointed out you'd get the photos for free.

Yes, your mom is a gem. Certainly, this time will be different. Today, once she meets your new romantic interest, she's bound to see exactly why you like them.

Why exactly do you like them so much, again? Oh yeah, forty incredible orgasms. Great. Glad you gave this so much thought.

The conversation starts with your mom asking, "How did you meet?"

"Online," you reply.

"Well doesn't everyone these days!" your mom says trying to contain her eye roll.

She continues with the standard questions, "Where are you from? Did you go to college? What classes did you take? Where do you work? What do your parents do for a living?" Then the bombshell, "What do you like about my son?"

You start to think of how they'll answer that question. What do you really know about them at this point? What would your answer be if their mom asked you that question?

For starters, they can do that thing with their tongue that you like. They make *a lot* of noise during orgasm. They slept in the wet spot. That was generous. They *didn't* freak out when you asked them to watch penguins in bikinis videos, so you could get turned on.

Your mom is still waiting for an answer. Their long pause is now growing into an uncomfortable silence and you can see them struggling to think of something appropriate. So finally, in what appears to be an attempt to end this deafening silence, they respond, "I like that he likes penguins."

Oh, hell no! penguins? You feel your face turning redder than old Aunt Stella's lipstick. Mom is staring at her, instantly judging, and probably thinking, "Well aren't you just filled with substance?" You can feel her disdain, instantly and almost tangibly, as she casts them into the "Just Another Fuck Buddy" category. Your partner is clearly trying to laugh it off as a joke while wanting to slither under the table.

Their face is now turning a lovely shade of bright red, not unlike your own, so you interject, "You are so funny. Always joking. I love your sense of humor." Whew, great redirect. Forget that it was *you* that put them in this situation.

Alternatively, perhaps you're a vegan and you take your new romantic interest home to meet your nature-loving, mushroom-eating, environmentalist family. Ten minutes into the meeting, your romantic interest is talking about how their family owns several cattle ranches and raises beef for the meat industry. Now they're talking about their monster truck *obsession* and just happen to mention how, for a laugh, they almost ran over twenty Save-The-Environment protestors.

Bet you're wishing they used their mouth for more conversations with *you,* instead of on your genitalia.

Maybe you have no less than fifty LGBTQ+ friends. These people mean the world to you. They are your very best friends, they've shown up for you and your family more times than you can count. Your life would be so much darker and harder without their light and love. You can't wait for your new romantic partner to meet all of them during dinner and a cabaret at a gay bar.

You walk in and are greeted with hugs and kisses from all your amazing friends. You turn to introduce them to your new beau, and you can see the horror and disgust written on your partner's face. They're homophobic! How did you miss that?

I'll tell you how.

You don't really get a comprehensive picture of who your love interest is with your faces and body parts buried inside of one another. Your gay friends are now being openly judged and hurt by this person's facial expressions and reactions. How could you do this? You immediately turn for the exit and text your friends your apologies.

You walk your partner to their car, and they tell you they would just like to go home… alone. They offer to arrange a ride for you.

You decline and decide to go back inside the venue to your friends, who immediately comfort you. They tell you that your new beau is an idiot, but they can't blame you because he's hot. Then they buy you an amazing cocktail and say reassuring things like, "Good for you for having forty orgasms this week!" Oh, how you love them.

You end up staying out all night with them and have the best night, as usual. On your way home, you realize your new romantic interest is not for you. You think about calling them; but what good will it do?

Over the next couple of days, you don't hear from them either, and realize they're also ghosting. This seems like the best path; there's nothing really left to say. Your community is incompatible with this person and nothing is going to change that.

Another scenario could be that you don't want children. You told your new friend this on your very first night together. They emphatically stated they were neutral on children themselves. You were so relieved because it's been an issue with other partners. They've invited you to meet their parents, and you are going to their home for lunch today.

When you arrive, you meet their brothers and a sister. Everyone is really nice, but you can't help noticing there are six kids bouncing around. They are cute, but *so* loud! You feel a migraine coming on instantly, but you try to smile through it.

You're relieved when their mom leads you to the back patio, where you can clearly see several bottles of wine. Ah, wine! Your happy place. You almost desperately grab the glass handed to you. With wine in hand, the parents start their interrogation.

Things seem to be going well. You've been honest and authentic; and so far, no one seems put off by you. You're feeling pretty optimistic about this visit. Just as you're settling in and starting to get comfortable, which also requires blocking out the sound of all those kids, the parents begin laying the groundwork.

They, not so casually, comment on how nice it will be when their last offspring has their own children, and you realize they're referring to your new love interest! As you practically choke on your wine, they continue. Excitedly, they elaborate on how the last person didn't like children at all. To nail the point home, mom says with great conviction, "Yeah, that's not someone who will fit in our family very well."

The wine you are drinking suddenly becomes very bitter, seemingly burning your throat. You start coughing uncontrollably. Subtle. This is going great, isn't it?

You regain your composure and drink some water, thinking they'll have forgotten what they were talking about before you almost drowned yourself in wine. Unfortunately, there's no such luck. As if to deliver the final knockout blow, the mom directly asks if you want children.

Before you can respond, your partner is answering for you. "We aren't really at that point yet. We're just getting to know one another."

You are stunned by their answer. You may have just met, but you've been very clear about your stance on children. Nonchalantly you interject, "I don't want children." By the look on everyone's faces, you might as well have said that you eat small children for breakfast. Their mom is almost in tears, dad consoling her, and your romantic interest has their hand over their face like you just admitted to sleeping with his best friend on your wedding day.

If judgment were a whip, you'd be bleeding out right about now. This is one of those moments where you are desperately wishing you'd spent more time assessing compatibility, conflict, and communication.

On the positive side, though, those forty orgasms have depleted your energy and the wine has added to your zen vibe, so you appear calm and level-headed. You realize that you definitely should have *communicated* about something more than oral sex and porn preferences the past two weeks. There's really nothing left to say or do, except collect your things, excuse yourself, and hightail it for the door.

There are so many other scenarios regarding community incompatibility.

For example, you like to watch football on Sundays, but their family has regular family get-togethers, without electronics. Can you imagine what this would be like for a sports fanatic?

It could be that you are a clean freak and like your home to be free of clutter, but their family has saved, literally, everything their entire lives. When you sat on the couch it was *sticky*! You almost gagged.

What if you don't drink, smoke, or do drugs, but when you visit their friends' apartment you feel like you just walked into an after-hours party in Miami. Everything in their home reeks of marijuana. Just sitting in their apartment, you're pretty sure you got high. You hope desperately that your employer doesn't perform a random drug test this month because you're convinced you wouldn't pass.

There are so many different scenarios we could explore within your community. We haven't even touched on politics, religion, vaccinations, race, or women's issues. All of these can be very divisive, and could easily derail a blooming relationship.

Your community can be a crucial C, depending on how important they are to you, and whether or not you share their viewpoint. *Their* compatibility, communication, and conflict resolution skills can also have a serious impact on your relationships.

You have to be honest with yourself and the people you are interested in long term. If you know that you and your new love interest differ in certain areas, then you should assess how these differences will be received by your community.

Is your community narrow-minded and judgmental; or are they open and accepting? Is your community really rooting for your relationship success; or do they have a history of being negative and petty no matter who you bring home?

Now, if someone is just a casual fling and you have no intentions of ever introducing them to anyone in your life, ok… carry on. Community is probably not that important to you in this case.

It could be that you're embarrassed of your family and you don't want to introduce them to anyone you're dating. If that's the case, then it's worth explaining this dynamic to your new beau. Otherwise, they might wonder if you're ashamed of *them*. Be honest with them about your inner circle. Talk through potential issues *before* placing each other in the shark tank.

I've often wondered, why is it so hard to be honest? Lying to people or concealing facts and information says more about your character than it does about the person you're interested in. You are the one causing drama with your dishonesty, because most people will figure it all out eventually.

So give people credit for being able to handle the truth. Someone that truly likes you and vibes with you might be willing to navigate these issues with you *and* your community. It doesn't matter if you are looking for a casual encounter or a life-long partner, be honest with all parties.

If someone doesn't like something you've represented about yourself or your inner circle, then let them go. Quit lying to people in the hopes that you will persuade them to stay or fit into your community. You're creating drama for everyone, and another shit show won't be far behind.

If you are looking to find peace, fun, and joy in your encounters or relationships, get used to verbalizing and walking in your truth. Not just the truth about yourself, but about your partner, and about your community.

Depending on how important it is that your partner fits in with your community, you might want to spend some time thinking about what type of person could realistically be a good fit. Are you seeing how this factor can enhance, or diminish your relationship? Choose wisely.

If you and your potential love interest have gotten through community introductions and you're still vibing, then you might be ready for the next C. Commitment.

If you're commitment phobic, this might be where you get sweaty palms and a stomach ache. Regardless of your stance on commitment, this next chapter can be very useful. Again, this book is about being the authentic, honest version of yourself. So, if no commitment is where you're at… that's ok. Just own your stance.

So, count to ten and let's talk about *Commitment*.

CHAPTER 8

The Sixth "C": Commitment

Whether you want a commitment or don't, figure it out and embrace your decision. If your decision is to remain single and have lots of great sex, then just state it. By giving people honesty and transparency, you allow them to make a decision that is best for them.

This might mean they pass on dating you. That's ok. It's better than creating confusion because they naturally develop emotions and feelings for you. Afterall, wasn't that why you were being so charming? Didn't you want them to like you? To sleep with you? Emotions are completely normal. We seem to forget that these days.

To reinforce an earlier point, do you start categorizing their feelings as drama? Did they create this situation, or did your dishonesty create the drama? When you mislead people about your stance on commitment, and then *drama* ensues, understand *you* are the one that started it.

It's your shit! Own the shit *you* created, and have some empathy.

The other party is entitled to have feelings and a reaction about your manipulation. They're human. Humans have emotions. It's not a defect. It's by design. So, if you want to minimize drama in your encounters, know what you are seeking. Then, own it, communicate it, and have fun with the population of people who are open to your perspective.

It all goes back to compatibility. Compatible relationship goals should minimize *conflicts,* which should minimize drama. Having a compatible stance on *commitment* is key in choosing who you spend your time with. If you are looking for a meaningful relationship where your love and efforts will be reciprocated, state it.

Have you ever dated someone and realized that you have feelings for them, but you're too afraid to let them know?

Let's think about that for a second. You met someone wonderful. You're falling in love with them. What a monumental feeling! How awesome is it that you have found someone that evokes those emotions? Shouldn't you be happy and celebrating that? At the very least, shouldn't you want to express it? Instead, you are fearful of rejection, hiding your insecurities, and anxious that past experiences will play out again.

I can't tell you how many times I've heard people express their fears, about love, instead of their joys. They meet someone they *finally* like, and now they're having anxiety attacks? It's like they go from orgasms to panic attacks.

Maybe your new person has already let you know that they are not interested in a relationship. You're heartbroken because you felt that you finally met *your* person. Instead of ending things, you hide the developing feelings and hope things will change. When they don't, you tell yourself to enjoy it for as long as you can bear it.

This sounds utterly miserable! How is this bringing joy and peace into your life?

In my opinion, unrequited love is toxic; and exactly where communication should come back into the equation. Good *communication* can lead to *commitment*. Maybe your love interest has also changed their position but hasn't figured out how to tell you. They may be surprised that they have developed feelings for you and may be struggling with how to tell you. Don't assume. Talk it out.

Regardless of which situation you find yourself in, your feelings are your truth. They may not be reciprocated, but no one should ever make you feel like you can't express your true feelings. Worse yet, no one should make you feel bad for developing those feelings.

It's understandable that you're hesitant to tell them, because expressing feelings, especially love, makes us vulnerable. What if they don't feel the same? It could end your relationship with this person.

The problem is, if you were looking for commitment, silence isn't going to bring you closer to realizing that goal. The longer you invest in someone that isn't investing in you, the longer you are keeping yourself from finding someone who will. This person is taking up space in your life that could be given to a better match.

It's like setting a goal to accomplish something and then not doing anything to make your goal materialize. For example, you set a goal to finish college so you can get a better job. However, rather than studying every day, you pass the time playing video games. Six years have now passed, and you're still playing video games in all of your spare time. You're still in the same dead-end job; not living the life that you desire. You're letting this habit hold you down.

The same is true for toxic relationships. They take up valuable time, emotions, and energy with no hope of ever being anything but toxic. There's no return on this type of investment. Why are you committed to it, when they aren't?

There are also many people who, for some reason, commit to their partner, and just let their dreams and life get sucked out of them. Their partner is not supportive or positive. These types of relationships drain your energy and joy. What's worse is you allow it to happen. The good news is it's an easy fix.

You can change the direction of your energy from negative to positive by changing your level of commitment to people who no longer bring you joy. That's right. With one decision, you can say, "I'm done. I'm moving on. I'm committing to my joy and happiness now. I'm committing to the pursuit of what my heart desires; and not allowing people to treat me like shit anymore. I'm not tolerating a low input relationship any longer."

Will it hurt to let this person go? Yup.

Will there be a void that you want to fill? Most likely.

Will you miss them even though they didn't bring you joy? Absolutely.

What you need to remember is this tough time won't last forever. It will pass, making room for joy and positive experiences in your life. As it fades, you'll find more space to connect with people who truly invest in you and your relationships. By surrounding yourself with positivity and uplifting experiences, you'll shift your energy from negative to positive.

You have a better chance of attracting positive people and energy when you are generating positive vibes. You will also be more selective about committing to someone when you are firmly committed to your peace, joy, and happiness.

Yes, it's easier said than done. Change can be scary, and the path to a better life often feels uncertain. Every day, remind yourself of your stance on commitment, trust the process, and be honest about what you want. Embrace the fear as part of the journey, knowing that it's leading you toward something better.

If you don't know what you want, then take a moment to define it. Afterall, how can you be honest with others about your views on commitment, if you don't even know what they are? Being clear about your commitment level will streamline your dating process and make it more enjoyable. If someone's outlook on commitment doesn't align with yours, expect conflict over how much commitment you're willing to give or withhold.

If you're ready for commitment and they're not, recognize that they don't deserve the level of commitment you're prepared to offer. Does this mean you have to erase them from your life like a bad tattoo you regretted the moment it was inked? That might be a little extreme. However, they don't have to hold the same level of importance and priority you've historically given. Prioritize yourself and watch the changes that occur.

Let's dive into some examples about commitment.

You have been single for a while now and haven't found someone who inspires you. You decide to set up a profile on a new dating app, with hopes that you'll have better luck than in the past. You open the app and start answering all the questions.

Height? Hmm. You're only 5'5". You've always been insecure about your height and know women like guys over six feet tall, so you type in 5'11". I mean it's not like she's going to notice immediately, right?

You're off to a great start. Go ahead and conceal that until the first meeting. She'll be so thrilled to hear your rationale for lying. Women love that.

Perhaps you're older and you like dating younger people, so you set your age to be ten years younger. You use photos that are fifteen years old, or place excessive filters on your photos. You believe you'll be able to perpetuate this misrepresentation far into the future because everyone says you don't look your age.

What is wrong with just stating your age? The right person isn't going to care. You're the one that cares. You're the one that's insecure about it. If you look younger, why not embrace it and be proud of it? If your relationship develops into something serious, you don't think your partner is going to know?

Would you rather be old, or a liar?

Your partner may start wondering what else you weren't honest about. Getting older is a fact of life. Being a liar is a choice. Most people usually consider lying a huge character flaw. All this effort to conceal your age to get the right person, only to lose their trust?

Now, where were we? Ah yes, filling out this dating profile. Let's define your *relationship goals*. So, what are you looking for?

You start to think, "I don't want a relationship; but if I set it to *something casual* I'm not going to attract quality. I don't want to come off as a fuckboy." You ponder whether you should set it to *looking for a relationship* and just deal with the consequences later. Right now, you just need to lure some attractive, disease-free candidates into your bed.

In the end, you opt for *something casual* and hope for the best.

Great! Let's get swiping. Within minutes, you have several viable options.

You scroll across someone very attractive and notice they have "*looking for a relationship*" selected as their relationship goal. They've also sent you a message complimenting the badass helicopter in your profile photo. However, they end the message saying that they wish you well in your search because they saw that *you* have "*something casual*" listed as *your* relationship goal. They tell you that it would not be a good match because you have incompatible relationship goals.

Your attraction for this person (chemistry), and your ego, compels you to try to win them over. You do your best to convince them it was an accident. They buy your lies and agree to meet you.

You meet for coffee and it's going well, but you're starving. There is a sushi place next door, so you ask if they'd like to extend your coffee into dinner. Impressive move. Now they think you're interested in them, rather than just hungry.

During dinner you have all the right answers. They ask you how long you've been single. You weren't exactly sure what to say, since you're still living with your girlfriend, even though things are a little rocky. You've been sleeping in the spare room, but you're far from single. You know you can't tell this person that. If you do, they will surely not go to bed with you. Your ego really couldn't take that. Not to mention, you're so lonely and horny.

So, you tell them you've been single for six months because that seems like a good amount of time. Who cares about the truth or their feelings? You just need to accomplish your mission, which is getting laid and feeding your ego.

Your first date ends and you finally get that kiss. Simply luscious. You're totally hooked and want to see them again, so you ask to see them the next day. They already have an engagement with some friends at a small housewarming party, *but* they go ahead and invite you. You enthusiastically agree. This is all going so well. You're doing a great job of convincing them that you're not a knucklehead.

At the party, you are very affectionate with them. Openly showing your enthusiasm in front of all their friends. You take them out on the balcony because you can't wait to kiss them again. It's fire! You're letting this person and all their friends know you're totally into them. Unfortunately, that's not exactly the truth, is it? You're just lonely, horny, and starved for affection.

On the flip side, the object of your attention and affection is reading your actions as if you're *truly* interested. This party can't end soon enough.

You get back to their place and it doesn't take long before you find yourselves in bed. You have amazing sex, all night long, until you're exhausted. It feels so good with them cuddled up next to you.

When you wake up, it's early morning, and you start to panic. You've been out all night. How are you going to explain this to your live-in girlfriend? You jump out of bed and head straight to the bathroom.

You must have woken them, because they're now in the shower with you. Kissing you. Oh hell! You pull away and beg your mind to come up with a good reason to leave.

You tell them you need to get home because you have a *dog*, and you need to take care of it. In actuality, the *dog* that you're referring to is not a dog at all. It's the woman that you've been living with for the past eight years, with whom you are no longer happy. You, again, conceal this piece of information because you're so hungry for someone to pay romantic attention to you.

You want to see them again, but you know you can't invite them to your home. So, you think of an alternative that will help you maintain the pretense. You invite them to your workplace to meet your coworkers and spend time with you there. This will give them the impression that you're not hiding them from your community. It will also help perpetuate your lie, that you are interested in commitment.

You continue this for weeks, and now they're asking to come to your place. You come up with another line of bullshit that will buy you some time. You tell them your kids are coming to stay for the summer. You're so proud of yourself. You've now found a way to get out of spending the night at their place, *and* given them a viable reason why they can't spend the night at yours. Now you can continue getting your cake and eating it too.

You start coming over to their place before your six thirty a.m. shift at work. This means you arrive at your love interest's home at three thirty in the morning! You want to make it look like you're such a great guy because you're making this *effort*. Again, it's a better narrative than, "I'm lonely, horny, and in a relationship!"

After a couple weeks of this, they eventually offer you a key to their apartment. They did this because they don't want to get up from a dead sleep to let you in. They also don't want to leave their door open as it's not safe. Giving you a key will allow you to let yourself in and wake them up nicely with kisses and putting your arms around them.

For whatever reason, though, the key symbolizes *commitment* to you. You panic. You just want your freedom and fun. So, you tell them to pump the brakes and not get so carried away. There's no reason to "lock shit down." You immediately start treating them indifferently. You withdraw. They're left wondering what happened. You're left trying to figure out how to get out of this.

You're supposed to pick them up from the airport after one of their business trips. You already made plans to go out together. When you pick them up from the airport, they are all dressed up and ready to enjoy the night with you. You intentionally show up in your shorts and a t-shirt. You tell them that you're not able to go out with them. They are crushed.

During the drive back to their apartment, you let it slip that you've *talked* to your ex. Your love interest is surprised by that because you talked so negatively about your ex in the past. Your new love interest asks you when you last saw your ex and you say "Wednesday." It is currently Friday. So, that was two days ago while your new paramour was away. Now, your new lover asks when you last had sex with your ex. You realize this is the out you've been looking for. You take it. You tell them, "Wednesday."

You further reveal that you still live with your ex and she is not really your ex. She is just someone you'd like to be your ex. However, you have been in a relationship for years.

Your new lover is devastated. They believed that you were emotionally available. They believed you were single. They believed that your kids were visiting for the summer. You misled them and lied to them.

Why?

The answer is simple. You wanted to get laid and fill the emotional void left from your dysfunctional relationship.

What level of commitment is this exactly? To whom were you committed? Your dick?

You were living with a woman who was part of your family for years! She cared about your children, your parents, and your friends.

You met another great person and dragged her into your dysfunctional life. What's worse is you made her an unknowing side piece. Something she would never have chosen for herself. Congratulations! You've ruined her trust for everyone that comes after you for quite some time.

You were in a toxic place and you used your new lover as an escape from your shitty relationship. You let your frail ego, low self-esteem, and selfishness take priority over integrity. How did you think that you could be a serious candidate for this new love interest? She made it very clear that she was not interested in a casual relationship. She certainly wouldn't knowingly put herself in the position of being *the other woman.* You didn't even give her the choice.

Now you're upset because there is *drama* and you can't get away from it fast enough. Drama that you are blaming on both of the women in your life. It's all *their* fault. Yes, these women are absolutely irrational and hysterical. Clearly!

How dare they have feelings for you! You didn't ask them to fall in love with you. It's not *your* fault you're so damn awesome. How can anyone be upset with *you*? You have needs.

You're just trying to get them met, so what? You told a little lie. What's the big deal?

The problem is that you're a selfish asshole and you need to embrace that. Refer to Chapter One. The Ugly You. This is your ugly part that you hide from others. How did hiding your stance on commitment work out for you?

Your new lover developed genuine feelings for you. She's compromised her integrity by being a mistress and she is hurt, angry, and upset. Not only is she upset with you, but she is genuinely upset with herself for potentially hurting another woman. Instead of apologizing, though, you gaslight her. You pretend that she is the one in the wrong. For what? I don't know. It's your narrative.

What I do know is that *you* should be upset with *yourself*. You should acknowledge how this all came to be. You were quite simply in an ugly place in your life that you weren't proud of. So, you blatantly lied to get what you wanted by withholding key facts about your ability to commit. Facts which would have let this person walk away right from the start.

For whatever reason, you couldn't face the ugliness about yourself and your situation. Your ego wasn't strong enough to stomach the truth, or the rejection. It was your shitty situation that *you* made worse for everyone around you. Of course, you'll never see it this way. You're a narcissist. So you'll continue to play the victim and blame others for your selfish behavior.

Let's explore another scenario.

So, here we are. Back on the dating apps. Swiping through a fresh round of viable candidates. You narrow your selection to a few people and you're ready to start the meeting phase of this operation. You suggest a "Netflix and chill" date to all of the options because you don't want to spend money on them; you're just trying to get laid.

Now, all of these options had "looking for a relationship" set as their goal. They all want to go out, on an actual date, with you. What the hell is wrong with these people? Why do they have to make it so difficult?! Clearly there is something wrong with *them*.

Why is everyone so down on the Netflix and chill thing? How bad can it be meeting a complete stranger on the internet? What's wrong with agreeing to go to someone's home for drinks *they* will be making for you? How else are you going to get them into the mood so that you can have casual sex with them?

Why is everyone being so cautious? It's not like anyone has ever been drugged, video-taped, and assaulted or murdered by an internet predator before. Everyone that you meet online is completely normal and emotionally stable. Right?

What you're actually looking for, here, is a free escort, but even escorts have rules to keep them safe. You just don't want to admit this is what you want. You don't like the sound of it. Besides, you want companionship and quality time too. It's just that, like Netflix, you want these things *on demand*.

You want people to fill the gaps in your already comfortable, full life when it suits you.

You are not interested in commitment. You are happy having the freedom to see multiple people. You like doing whatever you want without having to consider someone else's feelings about it.

There is absolutely nothing wrong with this. It's great that you know what you want. So, why are you hiding your truth from potential paramours? Is it hard for you to acknowledge this about yourself? Is it hard for you to say, "My life is full and I just want someone to fill a gap whenever it suits me"?

Maybe you don't like the candidates that are open to what you want. You want all the privileges that come with a relationship, without the obligation of one. There are lots of people who share your perspective on commitment. So, why go after the ones who don't?

One reason might be that you're actually looking for more than just sex. You've rationalized that people who are looking for relationships treat you better. You don't like being treated like a piece of meat. You're a good person, and you want substance. So, you've somehow concluded that you must lie about your position on commitment. You believe this will help lure better candidates.

Isn't this a very complicated way of achieving your objective?

Wouldn't it be easier if you start by being honest with *yourself*? If you can't stomach the truth and want to pretend you don't want on-demand sex, get an escort. Escorts will pretend to be whatever you want them to be for a night. If that doesn't appeal to you, then accept the population of people that have a compatible stance on commitment. Out of millions of people on the planet, surely you can find a suitable match.

You just have to start by being honest with yourself. Stop bitching about the *drama* in your interactions. Own that shit. *You're* the drama manufacturer. Stop shaming people who develop feelings for you and want more out of a relationship. Especially if you pursued them knowing full well they were looking for a more serious relationship.

The point here is to be clear about your intentions regarding commitment.

No one is saying you need to know at first glance that you want to be in a relationship with someone. However, you should know whether or not commitment is something you want at all.

Can you change your mind later? Of course. But you need to communicate when that change happens. Being honest and truthful throughout the entire process is really the best approach.

Now, some people can't handle the truth. Is that your problem or theirs? Your truth is your truth. Being honest with someone about where they stand in your life might be a hard conversation, but *communicating* it doesn't make you an asshole.

There are at least twenty different ways you could tell someone you're not interested in a commitment. Letting them know the truth can be a gift.

A gift? How can telling someone I only want casual sex be a gift?

Easy. You told them the truth and gave them the power to make a decision that was best for *them*. If you're worried about being an asshole, aren't you more of an asshole if you just lead them on?

Wow. What a concept. Empowering someone with the truth to take appropriate actions for *themselves.*

Being honest about commitment is a critical factor in getting what you want. It shows that you care about someone other than yourself. It shows that you have integrity.

People's beliefs and wishes about commitment seem to be a very hard topic to discuss. Whether they want it or not, there seems to be a lot of fear and anxiety about voicing their true feelings. How will you achieve or manifest your ideal state, if you can't even acknowledge it to yourself and others?

Be bold. Be brave. Be honest. Be yourself. Declare your truth. Consciously seek out others that have a *compatible* perspective. *Commit* to your position on *commitment.*

In anything that you desire to achieve in life, you have to commit to it in your mind. Your actions will follow your mind. It doesn't matter if it pertains to relationships, work, or just life in general. The narrative in our head is *everything.*

It can propel you to greater things, hold you in place, or drag you down. Your mindset is directly related to your level of commitment to anything. It drives our passion, our priorities, our actions and our *choices*.

Guess where we are going next? You know how this works. Let's talk about the last "C" in the selection process–Choices.

CHAPTER 9

The Seventh "C": Choices

C hoices. Choices. Choices. This is the C that I would consider the most powerful. It is also the one you have the most control over.

Dating gives us lots of opportunities to exercise *choice*. I mean, just think about it. If you're on a dating app, finding a person for whatever agenda you're trying to execute is like shopping for avocados these days.

What do I mean by that? Well, you can usually find a good avocado to take home and consume without performing an extensive assessment. When you're shopping for an avocado, you probably take a look at the pile of them. Then the selection process starts.

Do you want the California or the Florida ones? Perhaps you squeeze a couple of them a little to see how ripe they are. When you find the one that is the perfect level of ripeness for what you're making for dinner, that's it! You put it in your cart and you take it home.

Once you have it at home, you cut it open. That's where you find out if your decision-making process worked. Let's say you exercised bad judgment and your avocado has rotten spots inside. What do you do? You either throw it all out or carefully try to extract the good parts before discarding it.

However, if you choose a good avocado, it will be the most splendid shade of green inside. It will have the perfect level of firmness. It won't be too ripe, nor too hard. It's exceptionally creamy and luscious. Jackpot!

Now what? Easy! You throw away the shell and the pit and devour it. After all, tomorrow you can go back and get more. There are hundreds of other avocados waiting at the store for you, right?

Also, have you ever noticed avocados have a very limited shelf life? If you get busy and leave them for a few days, they go bad. No worries though. The store always has tons. So, you can just throw out this batch and go back to the store and choose some new ones.

Choices. Thanks to internet dating, we have a lot of them.

No matter which app you're swiping, there's always going to be a steady supply of new choices to take home. It also won't take you long to consume someone's good parts and then discard them. Said differently, there's always going to be more options to exercise and choices to make. However, when it comes to dating, we are dealing with people, not produce.

This perception of *endless options* has an effect on the choices we make in our interactions with potential romantic partners. For example, if you think your potential mate is only average, you might *not* be inclined to make the choice to invest in them or treat them well. Why? Because you're not that into them and you have FOMO (Fear of Missing Out). So, you're still on the dating app looking for a better option.

In life, the choices we make often drive the results we achieve. We can have sex with who we want. We can ghost who we want. We can have multiple people, simultaneously, if we want. We can choose not to resolve a conflict or apologize if we want. We can choose who to prioritize in our waiting rooms. We can even treat someone like complete and utter shit; the choice is ours.

Who cares about their feelings? We've got other options if they don't like it. Caring about someone's feelings is a *choice*. Knowing that you have a plethora of options can sometimes make us treat people as if they are disposable.

Perhaps you're on the other side of this type of behavior. If you are, understand there is nothing you did to deserve this, and it has nothing to do with you. This is also not something you can control or change. What you can control, however, is whether you *choose* to tolerate it.

Choosing to accept being treated like an option is up to you. Choosing to put another person's happiness and peace, over your own, is also up to you. If you are always the giver and the people you date are takers, it's your choice to accept that dynamic.

Sometimes, we can become so focused on choosing to make others happy or trying to impress them, we compromise our own values.

Set boundaries. You don't have to cater to anyone. It's your choice. Choose yourself and your peace. If someone doesn't respect you or disrupts your happiness, guess what? You have options. You can choose your own peace and happiness over entertaining anymore of their bullshit. Honestly, you're better off without them.

Let's explore this a little. You've been married for several years now. You're committed to this person. You declared your love for them. You even wrote your own vows!

Years later, you find yourself in a relationship where one, or both, of you is not living those vows. Now what? Do you stay or do you go?

What is the right choice?

You want so badly to resolve the issues and get things back to *normal*. The other party, however, is choosing a different path. They choose not to resolve the issues. Their future doesn't include you.

Let me tell you something. The hardest thing that I've ever had to do in a relationship that was failing was... nothing.

Yes. You read that right. Nothing.

Why would I do this? I recognized that they had made their choice and our relationship was not it. No amount of talking, compromising, pleading, or bargaining was going to change that. I had to be honest with myself and accept the outcome wasn't anything that I could control. My choice was only 50% of the equation. Unless the other party's *choice* was *compatible* with mine, we weren't going anywhere together.

In that moment, you might be replaying all the things they said to you on your wedding day, or any of the other numerous days that they declared their love for you. You might be saying, "Wow, that was all a lie." How will you ever believe anyone else again?

You will probably be changed by this experience, but change doesn't have to be a bad thing. After some reflection, you'll come to realize that you probably shouldn't have ever chosen this person in the first place.

I've been there many times. Looking back on those relationships, the only thing that I regret is not letting them go sooner. I deserved better. I wasted valuable time on people I would have nothing to do with today. I would make many different choices now.

When someone chooses to end a relationship, it can be tough. After some time, when you've processed your grief, you'll realize that person wasn't actually a great choice. You might recognize that there were signs long before that you ignored. Yet, you still chose to continue the relationship.

If you were honest with yourself, you might conclude that at the time you met them, you weren't a whole person. You met them at a moment of weakness. You met them when you were on the rebound, or afraid of being alone.

Fear of being alone can cause you to *choose* someone who's not actually that great.

Your friends all saw it, but you ignored them. You're starting to remember all the times those love interests treated you poorly. They gave you the silent treatment and called your family trash. They even convinced you to feel like you should be *lucky* they *chose* to be with you.

You even remember how they didn't like one of your children. Let's not even get into the years of bad sex you tolerated. For what? This wasn't your person. You had very few of the C's discussed in this book, but somehow you chose to be in a relationship with them?

Them choosing not to resolve things with you was a gift. Take it and run! Don't look back. Forgive yourself for your lapse in judgment, and endeavor to be more aware in the future.

Whatever the reason for that lapse in judgment, you've been given a new opportunity to find what is best for you. Make a more fulfilling choice; one that will bring joy and happiness back into your life. You learned a valuable lesson, celebrate that. Embrace this new moment in your life, and take all of the lessons you've collected to guide the choices you make now, and in the future.

Think about what choices will put *you* first. Reflect on what choices will support your truth, your happiness, your dreams, your desires, and most importantly, your *authenticity*. Give thought to choices that will make you shine, protect your peace, and lift yourself up. Don't you deserve to hold the priority spot in your life?

The choices we make, show love to ourselves. They nurture and protect us.

One thing I hear a lot from people who have children is that they have to put their kids first. I get it. I have kids. For years I tried to put myself first. I even tried convincing my kids that they were the neighbor's kids. Didn't work though. They still chose to live at my place and eat all my food. Apparently we look alike, so the "neighbor's kids" story wasn't working out. After a while, they grew on me, so I finally admitted that I was their "Mum."

The point is, even if you have kids, you still deserve to put yourself first.

When you are on an airplane, what does the pre-flight safety message say? "Put your *own* oxygen mask on before assisting others!" Even if those others are your children, make sure your own mask is on before you help them.

The positive energy and light that you will create by choosing to make yourself a priority and protecting your sanity is highly contagious. Your loved ones will benefit from the aura of self-love and light that is surrounding you. They will also benefit from the better choices you are making with potential love interests. So, choose *you,* my dear, and don't let anyone wreck your rainbow or make you feel guilty.

Another area where choices seem to affect our contentment in relationships is financial matters. We've all known people who have made a choice to financially depend on someone else. You can see very clearly that they are not treated well emotionally or physically, yet they choose to stay.

They are prioritizing financial security over their own happiness. You've often wondered why they're settling.

For some, it's easier to put up with a crappy relationship than it is to fill their own bank account. Being financially independent takes dedication, discipline, effort, drive, and commitment. Being in a shitty relationship takes tolerance. It's a choice.

Maybe you are this person. Whenever you start dating someone, you evaluate their bank account before any of their other characteristics. You might have all the other C's nailed down with this person, but you will never choose them. They can't provide the lifestyle you want. You have no intention of ever being financially independent.

You may have been in relationships already where this was the case. Your love interests grew tired of supporting you and your endless demands for things. So, they left. Each time, you became practically homeless and had to move in with friends or family. You've never lived on your own for any length of time. You'd hate that. You want to spend your money frivolously, not on rent, groceries, and wifi. This is what you choose.

Your current relationship is practically unbearable. You are definitely not sexually attracted to your lover. Every time you have sex, you're thinking of your hot, broke ex.

You have nothing in common with your current partner. To make matters worse, they have a bad temper. They say hurtful things to you when mad and you can't stand their family. However, they provide a car, a nice home, and tons of designer clothes. Things you consider *important*.

You know you are only with them because you are not financially independent. Going back to work or school is not an option. That nine to five life isn't for you.

Essentially, you are choosing to forgo all the other C's and your happiness to avoid working. You know this is what you are doing. You had explosive chemistry with your last lovers, and you don't have any of those feelings for your current partner. If only your past lovers had money.

Another scenario is choosing to date someone who has not resolved their past traumas and emotions. Maybe you're this person. You can't stand to be alone, but every time you're in a relationship with someone, you're constantly triggered and unhappy.

You're mainly brought together with your lovers through chemistry. As soon as things cool off and they stop spending time with you, you become inconsolable. You throw tantrums to get attention, but all that does is make them leave, permanently. You're choosing people to fill your voids rather than spending time healing yourself.

You are good at projecting an image to lure them in. You're attractive and you're a great sexter. You get them craving you physically. Like a drug. You're happy for a couple weeks while the chemistry is hot, and they keep coming around. However, once it falls off, you can't function.

Those closest to you know why no one stays in your life. They've tried to talk to you, but all their concerns are met with resistance. You don't want to be alone. No matter what you have to endure.

Perhaps you have been married for over fifteen years, with two children and a dog. Notice I didn't say *happily* married. Long gone are the days of *chemistry* that we discussed in the first chapter. You *wish* someone was having sex on your kitchen counter. Who knows? At this point, someone might be. It's just not you.

You can also forget about *commitment*, too. You have been cheating on your spouse for years now. You assume they are doing the same. The only *commitment* you have now is to your kids. *Commitment* to your spouse, at present, is relegated to paying your share of the bills. There is zero emotional commitment.

Compatibility is a thing of the past. You have grown into two completely different people. Sometimes you don't even recognize the person sleeping next to you. When did they start eating fast food anyway? The old you would never have married someone who didn't take care of themselves. Now, here you are, fifteen years later, sleeping next to such a person and they don't even put out!

Communication between the two of you these days is essentially less than you would expend on a frog. Unless you're me: I happen to love frogs.

Conflicts? Essentially these are really central to your relationship, at the moment. It seems you are never happy with each other. Nothing either of you does is good enough. There is always some criticism to be had. You argue constantly. When you're not arguing, you're just silent.

With respect to your *community*, they can tell something is off. The last holiday dinner was much quieter than usual. Let's just say the silences were uncomfortable for *everyone*.

After dinner, your spouse's tribe all congregated in the living room. You stayed in the kitchen pretending you were cleaning up. Really, you were polishing off that wine Aunt Marie brought to dinner. Thank you, Aunt Marie!

You have made the choice that you are not getting a divorce. You'll continue to have paramours to fill the physical and emotional voids you are experiencing in your marriage. You've been dating other people for years. You hide all of this from your spouse, children, and friends.

To make this all easier to swallow, you justify your actions with a story. You tell yourself that you spread good energy to your paramours. You leave them better than you found them.

You're honest with everyone you meet, telling them you are unhappily married, but you're choosing to stay, for the kids. Your honesty has made this a relatively drama-free situation. You have none of the C's with your spouse, so you choose to seek them elsewhere. You are content.

Your lovers, in turn, need to make a choice. They have to decide if this situation will work. Do they decline your offer? If they accept, it could mean missing out on someone they can truly build a life with.

However, you might meet someone who is in the same situation. A casual exchange is exactly what you both want. You could share great moments together and still be there for your kids.

By being honest with people, you empower them to make the best choice for themselves. This makes your encounters more positive and enjoyable. Isn't that the goal?

At the end of the day, no one but you can know what choices are right for you. My greatest hope is that you may see yourself in these examples and consider a more honest route that helps you embrace things you've been hiding; a better way forward filled with greater peace, joy, and love.

Love? Did someone mention love?

Whether you are seeking it or trying your best to avoid it, you have to admit, love is definitely an important factor in relationships... or is it?

CHAPTER 10

Love: Fantasy or Force?

Is love just a seductive fantasy, or does it wield real power over our lives and relationships? It might influence our chemistry and decisions, yet often feels insufficient on its own. Perhaps love is more a byproduct of the Seven C's, growing as we navigate them.

So, does love truly impact our choices and relationships? Can it really be the glue that holds us together, or is it merely a fleeting notion?

The answers are as unique as the scenarios. After all, you can love someone and not respect them. You can love someone and choose to walk away from them. You can love someone and recognize that they don't feel the same about you.

If love is powerful enough to keep people together, then why do so many people break up and feel sad afterwards? Wouldn't it be nice if, after you separated from a loved one, there was no hurt, pain, or loneliness? Instead, you'd wake up the next day and hit the "unlove" button… and voila! You're over it.

The definition of love is not the same for everyone. Some people show love through their actions, while others are good at verbalizing how they feel. Some acts of love are widely understood, like getting flowers; others are not understood at all.

How do you let someone know you love them? Do you tell them? Do you show them? Do you stick around like a golden retriever, drool all over them, and hope they'll figure it out? After all, you are so damn cute and you brought them that dirty stick sitting in the yard like a hundred times already.

I've made many mistakes in relationships, and the greatest was learning that everyone's definition of love is not the same. When someone says, "I love you," it can mean something totally different from your own definition.

Let's break it down in an example.

Imagine that you were raised in a "loving" home with two parents who were totally smitten with one another. They were romantic. They rarely fought. When they did, they talked it out and, fortunately or unfortunately, everyone in the house could hear when they made up. There was *way* too much PDA (public displays of affection) going on at all times. They also had each other's backs during times of struggle and endeavored to lift each other up.

This is the kind of love you've been searching for your whole life. Without knowing it, this example of love has been instrumental in formulating your definition of love and how it should be demonstrated.

You've dated others in the past, but it didn't work out because you felt the other person didn't really *love* you. The bar you have set for love is extremely high, based on what your parents demonstrated to you. You're not willing to settle for less.

Your parents also instilled in you and your siblings the importance of following rules, especially the rule of law. In fact, one time when you were in high school, one of your closest friends was arrested on a misdemeanor drug charge and your parents insisted that you cut ties with them. No matter how you pleaded with them to allow your friendship to continue, it was not negotiable. You eventually conceded because it just wasn't worth the conflict it was creating with your family.

Your last relationship recently ended badly because your significant other confessed that they were selling illegal drugs! You couldn't believe it when they told you. You were crushed.

You thought you had met the "love of your life." Your chemistry was on fire! You also enjoyed many of the same things, rarely fought, and always found a way to talk out conflicts.

Your family loved your partner, and although you've never met anyone in their family, their circle of friends was awesome. You were in a committed relationship for a couple of years. They were definitely the person that you chose as "your person." You thought they felt the same.

So, you couldn't believe that they were selling drugs and lying to you about it for months. What's worse was how easily they confessed it to you. They even made you feel like *you* should be *grateful* they were doing this. They seriously acted like they were doing you a favor.

This experience has really set you back because their explanation was just so sad and wrong. You're so confused, hurt, and disappointed.

So, what happened?

A few months ago, you fell on hard times financially and it took its toll on your mood and your spirit. You admit you were probably depressed because you wanted to provide for your love interest, based on how you were raised. You've seen it for decades, watching your own father, and you're committed to following his example. You want him to be proud of you.

Struggling financially consumed all of your thoughts and energy. You became very irritable. You didn't want to go out anymore because you had no money. Even walks on the beach were off the table because you didn't want to leave the house.

Your partner tried everything to lift your spirits, but nothing worked and they were worried about your mental health.

Your partner grew up very different from you. Their childhood was less than ideal. You see, many members of her family were drug dealers. As your partner got older, it was expected that she would also participate in the family business. Many times, your partner was left with random people while her parents disappeared for long periods of time due to incarceration.

Your partner told you when her parents were incarcerated, it was up to her and her siblings to fend for themselves. She knew that selling drugs was illegal but her family would tell her that if she *loved* them, she would do this for the family. When her family members didn't get the money they needed from drug sales, things got worse at home. Sometimes she even feared for her life.

It was like this her entire life, until she was old enough to leave and make her own decisions. It was only then, through extensive therapy, that she learned this was not how children should have been raised. Regardless, her own definition of love was formulated by these experiences. She grew up thinking making money from selling drugs was showing love.

So, when *you* fell on hard times, into despair, and all of her attempts to lift your spirits failed, she worried what would happen if you sank even further. Her life had shown her that it didn't matter if people claimed to *love* you. If they didn't have money, they could be monstrous to you and themselves.

She'd never seen you like this, and she panicked.

So, she contacted some old "friends" of hers and she started selling drugs again because she *loved* you. She wanted so desperately to make everything right again. She wanted nothing more than for you to be happy. If all that you needed was some money for everything to right itself, then she could easily solve this problem. After everything you had done for her, by taking care of her like no one else ever had, it was the least she could do to show her love and appreciation.

One night, she told you she had something very special planned for you. She made your favorite meal. She got all dressed up in an outfit you liked. Her hair and make-up were done so perfectly, she looked so beautiful, like a model. After dinner, dessert came. Let's just say it wasn't served on a plate.

In the aftermath of what you would have to admit was the best sex you and she had had in quite some time, she got up from the bed. Excitedly, she went into the closet, and came back with a box wrapped in gold paper with an exquisite black bow. Handing you the box, she said, "My love, I know these last few months have been hard. I want you to know I love you so much. You are the best thing that has ever happened to me. You've done so much for me and I wanted to repay the favor. Hopefully this gift can help you step out of this dark place you've been in."

You take the box from her beautifully manicured hands and open it. Inside is $10,000.

At first, you were elated. You felt all of the stress wash away. You could pay all the bills, buy some food, even get a haircut.

Then, just as quickly as the joy entered your body, the questions started flooding your brain like a storm surge in Miami during a hurricane. You felt an overwhelming sense of inadequacy because *you* should be the provider; and are totally confused about where all this money came from.

Before you could even stop yourself, you asked in an almost accusatory tone, "Where did you get all this money?" You felt your irritation rise. She replied, "Where do you think? I went out and I worked for it."

Without even asking for clarification, you knew exactly what she meant. Her part-time customer service job barely covered *her* expenses. You were the one that covered all the major bills. You were furious, not to mention disgusted.

After vomiting up all of your anger, disgust, and pain, you asked, "How could you do this to me? I *love* you so much. I thought you *loved* me too."

She answered, "I did this *for* you, because you were so sad. I was so worried about you. I thought you might take your own life. I did this for you *because* I love you, and I wanted to make it better."

Maybe we should pause for a moment.

Ready? Ok. Let's continue.

The purpose of this chapter is to challenge your assumptions about love and reveal its complex, varied meanings. The people you're connecting with may have had experiences that are worlds apart from your own, especially in their understanding of love. For some, love is the be-all and end-all of a relationship; for others, it's merely a minor component.

As you both fall deeper into love, don't just assume you're on the same page. Dive into a discussion about what love means to each of you. Uncovering these differences can either deepen your connection or expose cracks you never saw coming. More importantly, it may foster deeper empathy for another person's perspective on love.

Have you ever tried to define what love means to you? How do you show love? How do you interpret love? What does it mean for you to "be in love" with someone?

When relationships fail, oftentimes we hear, "They didn't love me." Are you sure they didn't love you? Is it possible the way they showed love was just foreign to you? Maybe they *were* showing you love every day, but you missed it because you were so married to your own definition of love.

I'm not saying that the way love was displayed by this person's girlfriend, in the example, was great, or that their relationship should stand. I am saying that we could try to have some empathy for her and not assume that she was a lying criminal. She didn't have ill intentions at all.

She grew up differently.

How love was shown to her clearly affected the way she was showing love in her relationships. It's also clear she put her boyfriend's interests before her own. After all, when did her emotional and physical well-being ever come first? I'll tell you when. When she met her boyfriend, who treated her so well.

She was so in love with him and so grateful for how he cared for her. She wanted to return those feelings. So, she did it the only way she knew. She put herself in harm's way, making her safety and freedom the last priority in order to solve their financial issues. A mind-blowing concept, isn't it?

So, how many definitions of love are there? Just think about how diverse and different everyone's childhood was. Add to that all of the different experiences a person can have with romantic partners over the course of their life, and you quickly start to see there must be millions of different definitions of love. Each person's definition is their own unique recipe, carefully crafted throughout their lives. What's yours?

Once I figured this part out, it really opened up my mind to different ways of showing and receiving love. I started paying attention to other ways love can manifest and be shown to me. This shift in mindset made me more grateful in situations where I previously would have felt unloved. While I'm still not going to tolerate certain things, I have more empathy and less anger when situations arise. The endings are also easier and more understandable to me.

There have been many books written on the ways men and women traditionally show love. It's definitely not a new concept that men were historically providers and protectors, while women were nurturers. At one point in our history, women were considered property and didn't even have a right to vote.

In the world we live today, things are not so aligned with traditional gender roles. We have a lot of single mothers providing and protecting because they were abandoned by the other parent. So, forgive them if they are not so nurturing.

We have a lot of men who stay home, as the primary caregiver for their children, because their spouse is off serving in the military. So, forgive them if they are not breadwinners.

We have women fighting for our country, who have taken an oath to serve and protect, not just their families, but yours too. So, forgive them if they don't wait for you to defend their honor when some guy grabs their ass in a bar. Just stand back and admire their awesome right hook.

There are men who openly show their emotions, and even cry in public. Shocking. After decades of being told to bottle up their emotions and be emotionally vacant, this should seem like progress. Yet, we often still refer to them as weak and tell them to toughen up.

There are also countless ways in which our community endorses our declaration of love as well. Some families will not believe you can love someone based on their sex, race, socio-economic status, political affiliation, or… football team.

Picture this: it's Sunday afternoon, and you've invited your new love interest over to watch the big game with your family. As you eagerly anticipate their arrival, your excitement is tempered by a twist—your date shows up in the rival team's jersey. Please tell me your family isn't shaking their heads. Your community is definitely going to question your love for this person. I mean, how could you? Were you even raised in this family?

Another factor that seems to contribute to how much you love someone is how much love you have for yourself.

It is hard to feel secure about how much someone loves you if you don't love yourself. If you look in the mirror and don't love the person that is looking back at you, how can you expect someone else to?

Now, maybe they will; but your insecurities will eventually creep in, causing you to sabotage a good relationship. Your self-loathing and emotional voids could suck the life out of them and your relationship.

Fill your cracks with self-love. Don't use other people as band-aids for what you are lacking. Another person shouldn't be expected to shoulder the responsibility of your happiness.

Work on being happy. Refer to that chapter on Choice.

Happiness *is* a choice. Loving yourself, your beauty and your ugliness, is one of those very powerful choices. Make it. You deserve to be loved by the most important person in your life… you!

The bottom line is that love is unique to everyone. Your love could be developed only by chemistry; or it could be developed with many facets and complexities. Love has many definitions. It's your show.

How do you want to love and be loved? Can you explain it to your love interests? Greater still, can you have empathy for *their* definition? While you may not hold the same definition as your partner, neither is wrong.

Love. Is it really the glue of a relationship? Only you can answer that question.

Well, we are approaching our final chapter. We have talked about the importance of knowing what we want. We have looked in the *truth mirror* through seven chapters of C's and learned there's a whole realm of things to consider besides sex. We've exposed all our ugly parts and realized it takes a lot of energy to hide them. Damn! Being ugly is hard!

Wait! Am I really ugly?

CHAPTER 11

Ugliness is in the Eyes of the Beholder

The first chapter of this book was entitled, "The Ugly You." You didn't think I was going to leave you with that thought imprinted on your brain, did you?

While we all have some undesirable characteristics, the most important "beholder of ugliness" is *you*. How you perceive yourself and how you let others define you matters profoundly in shaping your experiences and relationships.

Think about it for a moment. When we consider beauty, we often look to influencers, celebrities, or athletes, equating the term with physical attractiveness. Yet, Hollywood shows us that beauty, talent, success and money do not guarantee happiness or healthy relationships. If being drop dead gorgeous guarantees a great relationship, why do so many of their relationships fail? It's clear that looks alone are not enough.

The same is true for ugliness. Ugliness isn't just skin deep; it goes beyond what the eye can see. Many people come in attractive wrappers. Yet, underneath the glitz and glam can lie traits that obliterate their sexy exterior.

For example, cheating, lying, or being short-tempered can diminish anyone's attractiveness, no matter how beautiful they appear on the outside. However, some people may rationalize staying with someone solely because of their looks or out of fear they won't find someone equally attractive.

This overlooks what truly matters: character, integrity, and the ability to contribute positively to a relationship.

Ask yourself, "Is this really the kind of partner you envisioned for yourself?" Someone who might be good-looking but makes you miserable? If you find yourself constantly trying to please them or changing yourself, believing it will make them stop cheating or treat you better, you need to ask: at what cost?

Is it worth sacrificing your peace and self-worth for someone who does not appreciate or respect you?

Instead of chasing an image, take a moment to reflect on what you truly want. Go back to the fundamentals of how you define beauty and ugliness. Does it only include what you see? Or does it also consider your peace, joy, and sanity?

You might be taking full responsibility for everything that goes wrong in your relationship, defending your partner's actions to friends and family, and changing yourself to fit their ideals. But what about you? This person is projecting their own issues onto you, making you feel ugly.

Remember, it's not you, babe. You could be the most stunning person, have all your shit together, but it wouldn't matter. You could turn yourself inside out for them every minute of every day; but nothing would change. You can't change who they are or make them love you, and it's also not your responsibility.

Instead, shift your focus. Understand that their issues and ugliness have nothing to do with your worth. Their ugliness is just that... theirs. All you can control is your selection process and, most importantly, the value you place on yourself.

Stop looking for the right person and start becoming the right person for yourself. Embrace all your qualities, even the ones you don't like. Be the person you love when you look in the mirror. Then, go confidently into the dating pool abyss, without fear of exposing your "ugly parts," because there won't be any. Your self-love and acceptance will render any perceived flaws powerless.

Now, you may have some qualities that you feel compelled to change because you want to be a better version of yourself. Just make sure that you are making changes for the right reasons—because you want to, not because someone made you feel bad about them.

Be proud of yourself. If you don't like yourself, how can you expect someone else to? Own who you are and confidently show that to the world.

This concept is what inspired me to write this book. I want people to feel comfortable being upfront and honest about who they are.

After reflecting on my own failed relationships, I realized I often overlooked negative traits and doubted myself, trying to be better, smarter, prettier, and younger to keep someone's interest. I learned that if I wanted to succeed in future relationships, I needed to be authentic. I had to embrace who I was and share that with the world.

So, know this. You don't have to hide yourself to be beautiful. The most important thing is to accept yourself. What one person may consider ugly, another might find beautiful. Accept that you won't be right for everyone, and that's okay. There is someone out there right now who will value your unique qualities.

Embrace all parts of yourself, even those you've been hiding. By being authentic, you'll have a better chance of finding a partner who appreciates you for who you are.

I also realized that I needed to re-evaluate my selection process. When evaluating others, it's essential to look beyond just physical appearance, sex, and chemistry. These elements are just the surface.

This is where the Seven C's of Selection come in. Think of the Seven C's as if they were laid out like a report card. When you meet new people, try to assess them in each area before your emotion gates are fully opened and handed out freely. Take the time to consider these seven critical areas:

The 7 C's of Selection: Connection Considerations

Chemistry

- ✅ Attraction: Does the physical and emotional attraction meet expectations?
- ✅ Intimacy: Are they fulfilling your needs in the bedroom?
- ✅ Physical Chemistry: Is there a strong physical connection and desire?
- ✅ Emotional Bond: Do you feel a deep emotional connection with them?

Compatibility

- ✓ Shared Goals: Do you both envision similar outcomes for this relationship?
- ✓ Lifestyle Harmony: Are your daily lives and routines compatible?
- ✓ Interests: Do you have mutual hobbies and interests?
- ✓ Values Alignment: Are your core values and beliefs in sync?
- ✓ Future Plans: Do you agree on important future plans like family, career, and living arrangements?

Communication

- ✓ Style: Are you comfortable with their way of communicating?
- ✓ Understanding: Is there clear mutual understanding in your exchanges?
- ✓ Frustration: Does their communication style cause irritation or confusion?
- ✓ Conflict Resolution: Are you able to resolve disagreements constructively?
- ✓ Emotional Support: Do they provide adequate emotional support through their communication?

Conflict Resolution

- ✓ Problem-Solving: Do they contribute to resolving issues rather than escalating them?
- ✓ Responsibility: Are they accountable for their actions and capable of apologizing?
- ✓ Listening Skills: Do they genuinely listen and address your concerns?
- ✓ Stress Handling: How well do they manage stress and pressure in conflicts?
- ✓ Fairness: Do they approach conflicts with fairness and a willingness to compromise?

Community

- ✓ Friends and Family: Do they get along with your circle, and you with theirs?
- ✓ Shared Loyalties: Are your communities aligned on important topics such as sports team preferences, allegiance to schools, national identity, religion, political views, or women's rights issues?
- ✓ Social Integration: Do they integrate well into your social activities and events?
- ✓ Family Dynamics: How do they handle family dynamics and traditions?

Commitment

- ✓ Goals Alignment: Do their long-term relationship goals match yours?
- ✓ Life Space: Is there room in your life for them, considering your other commitments?
- ✓ Future Planning: Are you both willing to make plans for a future together?
- ✓ Investment: Are they equally invested in the relationship's growth and success?

Choices

- ✓ Priority vs. Option: Do they make you feel like a priority rather than an option?
- ✓ Time Management: Do they allocate time for you and your relationship?
- ✓ Support: Do their actions build you up and support your personal growth?
- ✓ Priorities Reflection: What do their choices reveal about their true priorities and values?

How many of us let our emotions get away before considering all the C's? Can you tell which C's you overlooked in past relationships? Would you have made different choices? If you had met their community, would you have still jumped in? Would you have walked away the first time they gave you the silent treatment?

Assessing the C's is not "one size fits all." What is important can only be determined by you. Each of us will place different levels of importance on each of these C's. Use them as a guide to enhance your selection process, so your encounters are more enjoyable and efficient.

Understand that you will also be evaluated by others and no two people will rate you the same. What someone likes or dislikes is unique to them. What stirs your emotions and drives your choices is composed of many factors and life experiences.

What is beautiful to you, may be ugly to someone else. That's okay. Embrace that diversity of opinion; it keeps things fun and interesting.

I've often been asked what I would have done differently in my romantic life if I had enhanced my selection process. The answer is simple, I wouldn't have chosen most of them. For those that remained, I would have left much sooner. I wasted valuable time I could have been using to find a more enjoyable match.

Next time someone rejects you or doesn't show interest, don't take it personally. Someone who isn't invested in you is doing you a huge favor by leaving. Let them go and take all their negativity with them! Don't spend valuable time and effort on people or things that don't align with what brings you peace and joy.

Find someone who celebrates and appreciates you. Choose a partner who makes you feel grateful for the journey, even if the destination isn't what you expected.

Ugliness is in the eyes of the beholder. Don't let anyone, including yourself, convince you otherwise. Love yourself, know yourself, and share that person with the world.

Look in the mirror and embrace what you see. You don't have to be perfect. You're going to spend a lifetime with the person staring back at you.

Last, but certainly not least, be proud of yourself. Give yourself some grace. You just might find that others will, too.

Glossary

Gaslighting: "A psychological manipulation tactic where one person causes another to doubt their own perceptions, memories, or understanding of events. It is a form of emotional abuse often employed to undermine someone's sense of reality". [1]

Ghosting: "The abrupt cessation of all communication with someone, such as a former romantic partner, typically without any explanation. This involves stopping all forms of contact, including phone calls and instant messages". [2]

Zombie'ing: "The phenomenon where someone who has previously ghosted you reappears after a period of weeks, months, or even years, resuming contact as if the previous absence never occurred". [3]

Love Bombing: "A tactic used to manipulate someone into a relationship through overwhelming gestures of affection and attention. This can include excessive flattery, frequent communication of feelings, giving unneeded gifts, and early discussions about the future. Although commonly associated with romantic relationships, it can also occur in familial and platonic relationships. Love bombing is often driven by the perpetrator's insecurities and need for control". [4]

Silent Treatment: "A form of non-verbal communication where an individual refuses to speak to another person as a means of avoiding conflict, expressing feelings inadequately, or as a method of punishment or control. This behavior can serve as a form of emotional abuse". [5]

Breadcrumbing: "A manipulative behavior in which an individual shows intermittent interest in a relationship, offering just enough attention or validation to keep the other person engaged without fully committing. This tactic is often used for personal gain or control". [6]

Endnotes

1. American Psychological Association. "What Is Gaslighting?" *Forbes*. Accessed August 6, 2024. https://www.forbes.com/health/mind/what-is-gaslighting/.

2. Merriam-Webster. "Ghosting Definition." *Merriam-Webster*. Accessed August 6, 2024. https://www.merriam-webster.com/dictionary/ghosting.

3. "Zombie'ing Explained." *Cosmopolitan UK*. Accessed August 6, 2024. https://www.cosmopolitan.com/uk/love-sex/relationships/a44837535/zombieing-explained/.

4. Cleveland Clinic. "Love Bombing Information." *Cleveland Clinic*. Accessed August 6, 2024. https://health.clevelandclinic.org/love-bombing.

5. Medical News Today. "Silent Treatment Explanation." *Medical News Today*. Accessed August 6, 2024. https://www.medicalnewstoday.com/articles/silent-treatment.

6. CNN. "Breadcrumbing Insight." *CNN*. Accessed August 6, 2024. https://www.cnn.com/2023/12/04/health/what-is-breadcrumbing-meaning-wellness/index.html.

Thank You For Reading My Book!

I really appreciate all of your feedback and
I love hearing what you have to say.

Please take two minutes now to leave a helpful review on Amazon letting me know what you thought of the book.

Thanks so much!

- Tanya